THE WONL
BUSES AND ~~TRAMS~~

Enthusiasm examined and illustrated
by
Jack Burton

For Robert & Barbara
With love
Jack B.

UNITED ENTHUSIASTS CLUB
2010

And when he saw the wagons which Joseph had sent to carry him, the spirit of Jacob....revived.

- Genesis 45 v.27

For the spirit of the living creature was in the wheels.

- Ezekiel 1 v.20

So he paid the fare.

- Jonah 1 v.3

The drama inherent in the simple ritual was evident even to an infant. First came the preparation, the impatient, expectant waiting. Then the driver walked into the road, opened the cab door, and climbed in. The bus rocked; the door slammed. The driver's outline filled the window, and his right hand reached behind to press the starter. The engine roared to life. The journey could begin....

Photographers and/or copyright holders *are credited individually. Unattributed photographs are from the author's collection and were taken by himself or by unknown photographers.*

Front cover: *The principal themes of this book are encapsulated neatly in this view of Eastern Counties' Bristol bus VG 5544 (LG 7) in St Giles' Street, Norwich circa 1938. Not only the bus, but the wonderful architectural variety, the signwriting and the period cars are all worthy of our enthusiasm, the whole focussed towards the tower and church of St Giles and everything it stands for. (Jarrold & Sons Ltd)*

Back cover: *City-bound traffic was held up in Maryhill Road, Glasgow, by a marching band, which gave the photographer a good opportunity to take this tram picture from the Forth and Clyde Canal aqueduct on 21st May 1961. By this date the tramway abandonment programme was well advanced, with Service 29 in its last few months. They were still very fine trams, even if their appearance was increasingly work-weary. (A E Bennett)*

Title page: *This is Norwich circa 1937. The trams have gone and, notwithstanding the many cyclists, motor traffic is developing its relentless stranglehold. Pride of place as we look up Prince of Wales Road goes to the two classically presented Bristol G-type buses of the Eastern Counties Omnibus Company. Every bus enthusiast of a certain age will recognise in this scene something of the origins of his own interests. (Jarrold & Sons Ltd)*

Published in 2010 by the United Enthusiasts Club
for the author at 7, Colegate, Norwich NR3 1BN
ISBN 978 0 9549659 1 4

CONTENTS

Here is a book for enthusiasts and for all who, at some time in their lives, have fallen under the spell of buses and trams. This can happen very easily, because buses and trams are big, noisy, friendly, colourful, reliable, familiar, reassuring, accessible, and essential. So step aboard for a journey with plenty to delight enthusiasts of all ages.

The book is set mainly in East Anglia, although Birmingham and Glasgow are featured too. But the setting is less important than the content.

I drove buses for thirty-five years, but they've captivated me for seventy. The child at the garage door always had my sympathy. Not only had I been there; I knew where enthusiasm could lead.

I've not travelled the world, but I've travelled up and down the streets of Norwich (my native city) in all seasons, mostly at the wheel of a double-decker. There are few better vantage-points from which to watch and learn. (And, when the cab was a half-cab, few better places to think).

Maybe this was my destiny. I never really wanted to do anything else. The die was cast long before schooldays began (in 1944). Like so many others - perhaps like you? - I was an infant enthusiast.

And this book celebrates enthusiasm! As you read, I hope you will feel that two enthusiasts - you and I - are sharing experiences; for I believe the things I have written will ring many bells.

But first, a definition. By 'enthusiasm' I mean any consuming interest or passion which grips our imagination and triggers a lifetime of enthralled pursuit. The spark can be ignited at any stage of life. A good companion may open our eyes to all kinds of wonders we had overlooked, yet which seem suddenly worth pursuing. But, often, enthusiasm can be traced to those earliest days, and seems to have lain latent and dormant before conscious thought began. This appears to be particularly true of buses and trams. Many an article, essay, and memoir has begun with fragmentary memories from childhood. Excellent! The tapes were fresh and clean, the world was bright and new. A quickening spirit was at work before we knew it. An 'interest' and affinity was being created; and I enjoy listening to such testimony.

Our enthusiasms are important. Not only do they enrich our lives to an incalculable degree by widening horizons, but they provide useful criteria which help us to compare and evaluate other far wider areas of our experience. This story, therefore, is about a little boy being born and growing up and exploring and interpreting the world around him. Essentially, it is the story of every child. This child adopted buses and trams as the pattern or template through which to interpret experience. Or, rather, it just happened - as most things do.

Never apologise for being an enthusiast. Don't be embarrassed. Be glad and grateful. However, to my particular tale there is a twist. If fate made me a bus driver, there must be easier paths to the driving school than the one I selected.

I abandoned the bus world to enter the sacred ministry of the church. When I was left hurt and disillusioned by my discovery of the way organised religion tends, sometimes, to function (inflexible, out of touch, obsessed with trivia, judgemental, disunited, less than honest) I didn't pack it in. Instead I won permission to become a worker-priest. Thereafter I was on bus driver's wages: but, at least, I no longer felt out of touch.

Again, this is not an apology! I mention these things only to avoid misunderstanding. But because religion interests me, it influences the way I express myself. I'm sure you can take that in your stride. You can be sure that this book is not a sectarian tract.

Yet if, by chance, as well as being a bus or tram enthusiast you are also a churchgoer - and there are many such among our ranks - it might occur to you, as you read, that this book could also be seen ͻus essay of a slightly different kind. If you felt like that I would be very glad.

ι, religion is primarily about doctrine and subjects like parables, miracles, and salvation, ͻu won't find God in these pages at all. (On the other hand, some may find reminders ͻf those themes, repeatedly.) To me, personally, a religious attitude to life means ꓦith blinking eyes, puzzling, wondering, worshipping. Religion - if it is about ꓦbout searching for meaning and pursuing dreams. If you believe that developing

2. The clock tower of Norwich's new City Hall peers over the rooftops to Castle Meadow, where Leyland TD4 AAH145 (AH241) heads for the railway station early in 1939. (Eastern Daily Press)

reverence, understanding, and sympathy are important, you may well catch here glimpses of God. If religion, to you, involves beauty, creativity, humility, hope, growth, death and disappointment, resurrection and new life - then here, in a secular framework, you will surely find echoes of such themes breaking through, over and over again (mostly without benefit of clergy or stained glass).

But none of it will happen if you cheat. Although there are no dull and obscure scriptural texts or quotations from the Fathers through which to wade, there *are* (for instance) a few very short lists of numbers. These are part of the story, part of the revelation, their sounds and shapes as important as my prose. They are intended to be recited. To read them slowly and silently will suffice; to skip them is to risk losing the blessing. See them, if you must, as my equivalent to the Old Testament 'begats' - but more interesting.

As an ordained minister of religion, I would be first to declare this essay void and inadequate were it not underpinned by genuine theological insight. It is. Those well versed in such matters will discern easily a comprehensive doctrine of Creation, which acknowledges God to be the Maker and the Keeper of all things, preserving and upholding from moment to moment, all that is: every living creature, every 'inanimate' object, every flower, every face, every trolley-pole.

They will recognise, moreover, a full-bodied doctrine of Incarnation - that God did not abhor, nor disdain to use, that which He had made and which He sustains - inviting us, thus, to search for whatever might bring light and sense to human existence, not in distant realms, nor in abstract philosophies, but among ourselves, in the world, in our daily intercourse with one another, and in the way we treat and handle the creation.

A few, possessing particular wisdom, might infer, thirdly - and how right they would be! - that the momentum behind any tentative progress I may have made in my restless searching enthusiasm is maintained and renewed constantly in thorough-going eucharistic doctr practice. Timetables and engineering manuals, for example, can bring enlightenment

3. The view over the bonnet from the saloon has enchanted generations of schoolchildren. Here in 1971 at the Edwards Road terminus of Norwich local Service 92A, they would have seen me in the cab, and my conductor Keith Burton changing the screen. (John Ray)

order: but - for me - the ultimate nourishment of the spirit takes me back to the Creation, for it proceeds from bread and wine.

But in the pages which follow, these matters are implied rather than stated. You must try to see it for yourself - and, even better, to feel it.

In *The Gap* (Triangle, SPCK, 1991, pp.72-73), I reflected on the way the universe prompts endless experiences of ecstasy, insight, and intuition - from a sunset to a barn owl. I continued:

'Similar revelations are experienced when humankind's creative mind wrestles with, tames and co-operates with the physical elements of the universe to produce new wonders: complex machinery; feats of engineering; computers; television. For many of us, especially those born before the age of the microchip, the shapes and lines, the designs and materials, which characterised the pioneering craftsmanship of earlier times, retain a peculiar potency: a windmill; a farm cart; an historic building; an old bus; a railway steam locomotive. Let no-one describe such wonders as lumps of old metal and wood which rot away! At one, mundane level they are - but they are incomparably more. They are all expressions of the creativity of the human spirit which wonders, probes, discovers, classifies, harnesses, and struggles to bring order out of chaos. They are testimonies to human endeavour: to that longing to know, to grow, to see beyond, to overcome, to be free. If any should ask: "What on earth has a steam engine to do with worship?" I reply: "It has everything to do with worship".

This book is a meditation on that paragraph. As such, it risks falling between several stools. It is emphatically not an autobiography - though much of it is presented in an autobiographical style. It is not an authoritative history or account of some facet of the public transport industry - like the monumental two-part *United* (Venture Publications, 2001, 2003), which I admire so greatly. It is certainly not, alas, a weighty tome of systematic theology. It is not even a considered account of my long worker-priest ministry.

It is an attempt to share my child-like, but fervent, belief that an interest, an enthusiasm, a hobby, or a ~~ ion is a wholesome thing - a lively colourful expression of the divine spark in each of us,
~~s to understand: longs to explore, relate, and connect; longs ultimately, above all, to love.
~~ of good-quality public transport is a mark of a civilized society - which makes trams
~~cularly worthy of study and research! But it might be cycling, match-box collecting,
~~ort, or singing: a genuine enthusiast will enrich not only his own life, but will touch
~~ who watch his pursuits and enthusiasms with sympathy, or answer his endless
~~ed curiosity and patience.

For all those reasons, I have attempted to evoke the secret heart of enthusiasm as I have experienced it, with its times of utter bewilderment and its special moments of bliss, wonder, passion and discovery. I have tried to illustrate the journey it involves, and the growth which occurs as the vision is pursued. I have paused to record thoughts, coincidences, laughter, and examples of symmetry which, occasionally, can seem so extraordinary they leave us looking for meaning - even when, probably, there is none.

But wait a moment! That word 'enthusiasm' comes from the Greek *'enthousiazein'*, which means to be possessed by a god, or inspired by a god. *'Theos'* (God) is plainly at the heart of enthusiasm, and an enthusiast is one who displays a God-inspired zeal. So let's not be too defensive. Any worthwhile enthusiasm, honestly pursued, is a religious activity - and from it we should expect the fulfilment and stimulation which religion, at its best, never fails to supply.

My essay also includes stories and memories told to me by men and women who had spent a lifetime in the bus industry. All this material was gathered first-hand from people I knew personally, in relationships which sometimes (on my part) grew from colleagueship into pastoral responsibility. These stories of great men who had gone before me are a vital ingredient in the narrative, giving enthusiasm a context, a background, a history, a continuity, a sense of tradition, and a sense of belonging. Far from being extraneous distractions, they are my Kings and Chronicles and Acts of the Apostles, and form the very life-blood of enthusiasm.

It is this quality of quiet awareness which can raise the cash-office into a cathedral, an oily pit into an anchorite's cell, and make the cab a retreat. But I haven't spelt it all out. I hope (and believe) that a thoughtful review of the enthusiasm which took root in one small boy before he was aware of the fact, and developed to become a decisive factor in his life, will generate insight no less valid for being implicit and not stated. Again, you must work it out for yourself.

My theme goes beyond 'hobbies' and 'interests'. The fact, or quality, which I call 'enthusiasm' - which includes an awareness of history and tradition; the satisfaction of 'old-fashioned' virtues like doing a job conscientiously; and the concept of 'service' (as in the now obsolete, alas, 'Public Service Vehicle') - is what ennobles all human labour, and enables us to look for God where Christ's Incarnation teaches us to look for him first: in the daily round and the common task.

Meanwhile, I hasten to acknowledge all the help I have received in preparing this little book. My daughter, Jeanette Burton, has spent endless hours deciphering my scribble and preparing a legible manuscript. Many people have answered questions, confirming and correcting my memories. My son,Trevor Burton, has given wise counsel.Any errors that persist are mine alone.

I record with particular gratitude and affection my immense indebtedness to my friend of thirty years, Philip Battersby, of Middlesbrough. He is a hard task-master who sets, by example, standards of research and presentation which, for most of us, are unattainably high; but he has been a constant source of inspiration and information.

Philip is an acknowledged authority on United Automobile Services Limited; also, he possesses extensive knowledge of British tramway systems, not least that of Glasgow Corporation. There is not a theme or thought in these pages that we have not explored together, at some time over the years; and he, too, has experienced the challenges and the demands of worker-priest ministry. When I suffered a stroke and was in hospital he sent me improving literature almost daily. It was usually a picture of an early United bus, or a Coronation car, or a United BBE (a type he knew I liked) bound either for Lowestoft or Glasgow. And, soon, I was much improved.

I now thank him and Angus Bell for preparing these pages, Harold Chapman and Saxon Digital Services for printing them, and all who have permitted the use of their pictures or texts.

But above all I offer thanks to:

MOLLY

my wife.

Nobody could have combined simultaneously the roles of minister's wife, busman's wife and sheriff's lady more effectively and naturally, nor won greater acceptance, affection and love.

Jack

Colegate, Norwich

1. Genesis

Perhaps I heard them in the womb. It's not impossible. The front bedroom in which I was born possessed (and retains, in my memory) two dominant characteristics. Because the slopes that fringe the eastern edge of the city gave to our small terraced house in Norwich an elevated outlook, the cathedral spire was visible and the sun set behind it.

Moreover, the house was on a bus route. During the day, the Service 92 zig-zagged its way up the hill at full throttle every ten minutes or so (then back down again, more cautiously). Maybe the confident roar of a Gardner engine sent waves through the protective waters that enveloped me, and in which I was preparing for my mission to sort everything out in the world which awaited my coming with bated breath. (Looking back, it occurs to me that perhaps it was Hitler's coming they were awaiting....)

Anyhow, I was aware of the Leyland TD4s from the beginning - I knew them as I knew my mother. I didn't know - couldn't know - many facts about them. The facts would come later, in a trickle; they would not come all at once. The words to express these things would also come later, also in a trickle - a much slower trickle, for I am still searching for the ones which might capture the heart of the matter.

I was learning that there are many kinds of knowledge. And I knew those TD4s. If not in the womb, then definitely from the window and the perambulator was I able to establish and acknowledge my relationship to them. That 'awareness' is the deepest knowledge of all. A fool can obtain facts; the knowledge I possessed was of a different order - it was fundamental, basic, intimate, sensual. I could almost say carnal if it didn't sound nonsensical.

There was nothing between us. I knew, even as I was known. I was them and they were me. We belonged on the hill together. Other people knew when they were due, how late they were, how the services were to be revised. But they didn't know them, nor relate to them, as I did. How could they?

I knew, then - though the words hadn't come, nor the notion consciously formed - that my kind of knowledge was the kind that matters most, and that my kinship with them was something precious and beautiful beyond price. When, later, some mocked my infatuation, I was unmoved and could forgive them. They didn't know. They couldn't help it.

The learning of facts (as distinct from establishing an emotional relationship) began early, though the two - for me - formed one natural, seamless robe. An autumn child, I emerged from those wave-filled waters in October 1939. One of my earliest memories is of being held at that bedroom window and seeing, on my right, blue double-decker buses (it may only have been one, but I imagine two) standing in the playground of the school at the top of the hill (and on the other side of the road, in the same frame as the cathedral spire).

It was not the mere fact that I saw buses that registered most deeply, nor that they were at a slightly unusual angle. It was the fact that they were blue, which tends to confirm that I was already familiar with red or grey double-deckers (for some of my buses were in the dull, grey wartime livery). Michael Glasheen, the boy next door, who was much older and whom I idolised, told me later - with all the authority that comes with advanced years - that the red ones had the best engines.

Some years afterwards, when I related this memory, it was explained to me that half of the school buildings (housing the Junior School) had been destroyed in one of the Baedeker bombing raids of April 1942. (Hence the prefabs, which housed the junior girls, when I started infant school in 1944; and the fact that when I moved to the junior boys' school in 1947, it was to another site, to classrooms which had been appropriated from the adjoining senior boys' and girls' schools.)

Th‌ ̶ ̶ ̶ ̶ue buses belonged to Great Yarmouth Corporation, and had brought workmen to clear the ̶ ̶ ̶ged site. The precise dates of these observations cannot be determined for certain, but ̶ ̶ ̶n is so important, it seems likely that action would have been taken sooner rather than

wonderful pieces of confirming evidence which, sometimes, come years after the ̶ ̶ ̶ly out of the blue, occurred on Tuesday 16th March 1982 when I spoke on 'Birds, ̶ ̶ ̶t a meeting in the village hall at Freethorpe, a village between Norwich and

4. From my childhood home on the slopes of Thorpe Hamlet, these Leyland TD4s were my introduction to buses, as they daily climbed the hill on Service 92 to Harvey Lane and Thunder Lane. In this picture, taken in about 1950, AAH 139 (AH 235) was reversing from Harvey Lane into Morse Avenue. As you turn the pages, you can presume that street names or local districts are in Norwich unless otherwise specified.

5. Great Yarmouth Corporation's EX 5012 (12) in their blue and cream livery was new in 1939, so it is not impossible that it was what I saw that day in Norwich in 1942. This particular bus was a Leyland TD5 with 48-seat Massey body, and ran until 1959. (R H G Simpson)

Great Yarmouth. I happened to include this recollection. Afterwards, an old man approached me and said he knew I was speaking the truth because he came up on those buses, which went round the villages, collecting workers, on the way to Norwich.

In another wartime memory, I recall being at Orford Place in a grey single-decker with an open, sliding roof vent, and sitting on (what was to me) luxurious blue upholstery. Note, again, it's the *difference* which registers; the normal seat-covering was a sturdy red and black floral design. (I have a sample on a stool I salvaged from the office of the operating foreman.) I think mother and I were returning from visiting my grandparents at Earlham, and the bus must have been an LJ - one of the 1936-37 express coaches relegated to more mundane duties for the duration of the war.

I recall the thrill of seeing - for the first time - an LJ freshly painted in post-war, cream-and-red coach livery, on Thorpe Road, around 1946.

Though I didn't know it at the time, my precious TD4s had been purchased for tram replacement at Norwich in 1935. When I worked for the Company at its Main Works as clerk to the Works Superintendent (1957-59), I found a superb photograph tucked away in a drawer which, to my astonishment, showed a line-up of six of my favourite buses in pristine condition, immediately prior to entering service. It was one of those moments of discovery which transforms and casts its spell over the entire day. The registration numbers of that batch of ten remain, to me, like mystical symbols - as, indeed, are all the registration numbers of the Eastern Counties fleet of my childhood. At that time, of course, this still included some which would have sounded vaguely familiar to United enthusiasts. Although they had been rebodied, several vehicles I knew very well - VF 8521 for example - had indeed started life as part of the fleet of United - for that company, having originated in East Anglia, had contributed its Norfolk and Suffolk operations to form one of the four constituent elements in the newly-created Eastern Counties Omnibus Company Limited, in 1931.

I want to emphasise this point. The very shapes of the numbers of the vehicles in the fleet during my boyhood seemed to hold a secret significance, like carvings on some ancient stone or sacred runes. Those of my TD4s, running in a short, smooth sequence, had particular potency. (The numbers which I discovered, in my teens, of vehicles in the original fleet list, or which had been obtained, operated, and disposed of before I came on the scene were the most amazing of all, containing meanings I still struggle to interpret.)

It is important that, here, I insert into this record the shapes which represented to me, as a small child, the rightness of things; the way, the truth and the life; the assurance that all was well with the world. I knew these numbers as I knew the names of all our neighbours, and with the same confidence that I could recite my address:

> AAH 136
> AAH 137
> AAH 138
> AAH 139
> AAH 140
> AAH 141
> AAH 142
> AAH 143
> AAH 144
> AAH 145.

Simply to stare at that list is to experience a fulfilment which is deep and reassuring. The creatures to whom those numbers relate spoke to me before I could respond. They offered a prevenient grace. I_____ ____ 'y worship was absolute and unquestioning.

_____ ____gan by operating on Service 80 from Earlham Road to Thorpe Road and up Harvey
_____ ____ been switched to Service 92 Mile Cross (Boundary Inn) or Catton Grove (Park
_____ ____ Lane (Morse Avenue - the same terminus as the 80 but approached from the
_____ ____ or Thunder Lane (Corner), via Plumstead Road (and our house), by the time I was

6. *This rare wartime picture of a 1937 BVF-registered Bristol JO5G coach, painted grey and relegated to ordinary bus duties, vindicates my early memory of travelling on one of them. In this view it was a bright sunny day by the Norwich Central Library, but not warm enough for the sliding sunshine roof to be open, and the bus edged its way through the crowds, the driver no doubt very conscious of the traffic policeman alongside. (Arnold F Kent)*

7. *Here is the photograph of six of the Leyland TD4s which occasioned that great moment of discovery! They were registered AAH 136 to 141, but (inconsiderately) were not lined up in that order when photographed at Main Works prior to entering service in July 1935. (ECOC Ltd)*

8. In their later years, the TD4s wandered further afield. Here AAH 137 (AH 233) was loading in the Norwich bus station in Surrey Street on Service 7 to Yarmouth. The 'relief' car - operators elsewhere used terms like 'duplicate', 'special' or 'extra' - was VF 8521 (AH 286), a TD1 which had been rebodied in January 1939 and went on to become the last former United bus in the Eastern Counties fleet. (Roger Harrison)

Other vehicles augmented the TD4s - but the latter had made the route their own. Single-deckers appeared only as lunch-hour ("dinner-time") workers' reliefs, or *in extremis*. For example, if there had been a heavy snowfall, the 'deckers would be withdrawn after tea and the evening service operated by saloons, which were deemed safer on the hills. I expect I am thinking of early 1947. The snow made the world different and exciting: but the single-deckers looked out of place.

Service 92 belonged to the TD4s, and I lived on Service 92. (The route number, too, assumed a magical resonance, which has persisted.) AAH 136, AAH 137 - it was a creed, a profession of faith. I suffered for them when they crawled past in thick fog. When the first one went up the hill in the morning, I knew it was about 6.30 and the night was nearly over. It was a welcome sound if fever or toothache had made the night long or if the new day held some special treat. If it was winter and still dark, and I was snug and warm, it more resembled a dire warning. If I was still awake around 11 o'clock at night and heard a bus go past, it was as good as evening prayer, and a benediction on the day.

Why me? Other people heard them, saw them, used them. Why did the buses take root in my sub-conscious mind the way they did, then blossom into consciousness (as I grew in self-awareness), already fixed confidently *in situ*, a secret knowledge, to which only outer, external, historical details had to be added? (When these were supplied, they added breathless and wonderful new dimensions to a pre-existent relationship.) But why me?

Perhaps God chooses some of us to receive this special knowledge. All receive latent gifts and abilities: maybe this is no different. We don't all respond to (apparently) similar stimuli in the same way. From comparable backgrounds, we don't all decide to be doctors, dentists, or secretaries. Siblings don't all flock into the same trade.

This instinctive feeling for buses and trams manifests itself profoundly in only relatively few people - though a surprisingly large number are responsive and interested, to a lesser degree. The phenomenon is one of those talents which - because it impinges upon so many other disciplines and

9. This view from City Hall c.1950 looks across the city of Norwich to Mousehold Heath on the horizon (where the Victorians built the barracks and the prison). In the foreground, between the market stalls and Jarrolds' department store, two buses complete a typical Norwich scene of the period. Advertisements suggest the vehicles could be AVF 352 (HLG 10) and BNG 204 (HLG 22). The ornate building on the left is the Guildhall. (Eastern Daily Press)

aspects of society - is capable of providing enormous enrichment and pleasure. History, engineering, sociology, economics, geography, investigative detective work - transport touches and relates to them all, and a knowledgeable enthusiast is a thing of beauty: or, at least, of curiosity and delight.

Buses and trams provide one - obviously not the only one - but certainly one distinctive and powerful model for the interpretation of experience, and the exploration into God, the Source of all meaning and being. For some, religion is the exclusive model. For many, it is music. It might be astronomy, mathematics, or natural history. For me, light comes from them all. But before I could say the 'Our Father', recognise a big end from a steering wheel, hum 'Riding on top of the car', read a graph showing profit and loss, know the difference between Aylsham and Auchenshuggle, or trace my own family tree (let alone the history of acquired operators), a knowledge and a relationship burned within me, gently but strongly; and, swiftly, were fanned to a flame.

But how bewildering the steps along the way! The love, the fascination, the commitment were all present: but the understanding - the earthly, human, mortal part of the process - was often painful and confusing. Invariably, the journey was intriguing; simultaneously, it was alarming: it threw open doors to fresh knowledge - which brought with it, always, new problems.

As she had carried me in her wave-filled waters, it was fitting that mother should be the agent of my second birth. The event to which I allude was an undoubted Epiphany moment - a manifestation, a revelation, a true shewing forth. I can think of several others of immense significance; these, too, I will describe in due course. But none matches the importance of this original Epiphany, which opened, for me, the door by which I was given access to a new and higher dimension of understanding.

I cannot pretend to put a date on this experience, but it was early enough for the TD4s to be working virtually every car-line on Service 92. There were no Bristols.

I copied the runes constantly. One dull afternoon, I watched by the window in the front room and compiled my list as the buses passed - roaring up the road, returning down more sedately. Each registration was noted. Then my mother dropped a bombshell. As one bus charged up the hill, and I duly noted AAH 137 (or one of the others - I can't

10. The alteration in the appearance of the early LG-class buses when the cabs were rebuilt was one of the details which caught my interest in those early days. The purpose of the alteration was to increase the space between the windscreen and the steering wheel. The rebuilt (and by then reclassified) VG 5545 (HLG 8) was photographed at the Neville Street bus stop on Unthank Road in 1951. (Roger Harrison)

remember which), mother asked - with that irritating blend of innocence, pertinence, curiosity and provocation at which mothers excel: 'What's that number on the side?'

I hesitated before replying. I considered her question gravely and courteously. Then I admitted that I'd never noticed a number on the side! We waited - and, in those days, not for very long. Along came (I believe) AAH 145. This time, I looked - and I saw it. Beside the driver's door, as plain as anything, was a number different from the one I always noted: AH 241.

An unexpected knock had been delivered to my status as an expert, for I had no explanation to offer. I had discovered fleet numbers.

Investigations, research, further observations and specific inquiries were put in hand - but it wasn't plain sailing. I concluded, fairly quickly, that the apparent connection between AAH and AH was an unfortunate coincidence and a misleading clue for, upon inspection, other double-deckers familiar to me, with exciting and satisfying runes like VF 8521, ER 8805, FL 8905, DX 9021, XV 3774 were found also to possess "side numbers" - as I called them - beginning AH. The AAH/AH link, which had seemed so obviously meaningful, was not meaningful after all, but mere chance, hazard, and coincidence, lacking any specific or special significance.

After Monday morning school, I made a point of waiting for the dinner-time single-decker relief. CVF 837 appeared. I looked for the side number. Yes - there was one. Was it AH? No! It was LL. LL 37. Now, there were two numbers to collect. If only they would go past more slowly.

Knowledge had advanced one step forward, even if (as yet) it was accompanied by little understanding. Most single-deckers had 'side numbers' beginning LL: but gradually I noticed different letters being used, like P, LN, and LD. Some double-deckers I expected to be AHs turned out to possess only a solitary A in their number, which looked strange. It was a long time before anybody told me that the H in an Eastern Counties fleet number signified a highbridge vehicle i.e. one not suitable for any route which passed under a bridge with headroom of less than 14ft 6in. Eventually, a trained eye meant I could pick out the slight squatness of a lowbridge car immediately.

11. In the same year VG 5543 (HLG 6), which avoided the 1947 cab reconstruction that affected its seven sister vehicles, was seen in Thorpe Station yard on Service 81 to The Oval. (Roger Harrison)

Other double-deckers bore the letters LG. These buses didn't all look the same shape. Included in this class were my second favourite vehicles. These, too, must be recorded individually, so great was their impact on my ever-expanding awareness:

VG 5538 (LG 1)

VG 5539 (LG 2)

VG 5540 (LG 3)

VG 5541 (LG 4)

VG 5542 (LG 5)

VG 5543 (LG 6)

VG 5544 (LG 7)

VG 5545 (LG 8)

Look at them! Aren't they magnificent numbers? For me, none of the magic has waned, sixty years later. They could always be found on Service 89. They were never on Service 92.

At the time, I had no notion whatsoever of their provenance, but they had originally belonged to the Norwich Electric Tramways Company. Their appearance altered slightly, at one stage. Later, I discovered that their cabs had been rebuilt in about 1947 - except LG 6, which still looked 'right' (though I liked the other seven also). An anomalous oversight was corrected when the 'LG' was amended to 'HLG' in 1950; and there was great excitement in 1952 when HLG 4 and HLG 6 were converted to open-toppers for use on the Felixstowe sea-front service - but nobody bothered to remove the 'H' added so recently to their fleet numbers. HLG 6 had its cab rebuilt only after it had appeared as an open-topper. I went (by bus!) with a friend to Felixstowe to see them.

Thus, gradually, this fascination which would develop into a life-long love affair, emerged from God. It was a new creation, as much part of me as hands and feet and self-awareness; and it began to develop, explore, and push back the frontiers of experience and understanding. Every sense was affected. The scent of a new timetable was, itself, a revelation, before ever its contents had been examined, while the three Beadle-bodied Bristol coaches of 1949 were an essay in beauty.

When adults divined this strange, childish interest, they themselves responded (though not with the passion of true believers, of course). Sub-consciously, they found they were slightly interested too, and being old, had fragments of faded memories, half truths, accurate recollections, and first-hand experience which they took pleasure in sharing. In equal measure, I took pleasure in receiving; but those revelations of pre-existent phenomena and ancient traditions were mysterious and mystifying - almost unmanageable, for they were outside my immediate conscious experience. (Irritatingly, most things were.)

Incredibly, it seemed there was a time before Eastern Counties. Apparently, in that period of pre-history, buses existed - but they were operated by an entity called 'The United'. The coincidence of the name caught my attention for in that early post-war period I had begun to notice coaches operated by 'United' sharing our Newcastle service. Obviously, there could be no connection, since these came from a place called Darlington, and even I knew that Darlington was too far away to be relevant.

Plainly, this was another red herring.

However, I was very interested in the United of which the grown-ups talked, and sensed it had to be relevant to the local bus tradition I was trying to unravel, absorb, become part of, appropriate, and master. History interested me and, even as a child, I realised that, although I myself dated only from 1939 (and despite Eastern Counties being one of the fixed points in my universe), 1931 was not, in historical terms, very much further back. Shakespeare was *much* further back; William the Conqueror even further back: (he was 1066); and the Romans and Jesus were further back still. There seemed a strong possibility that the grown-ups' United might be part of the story - indeed, might be the missing dimension, the factor which could go a long way towards filling annoying gaps in my present understanding.

For example: Eastern Counties Service 7 operated from Norwich to Great Yarmouth via Blofield and Acle; Service 7B left the city via Yarmouth Road but turned off at Blofield and operated to the villages of Pedham and Panxworth. But why that gap? - why 7B? One day, amid a host of adult United recollections, my ears pricked up at a reference to the 7A. It ran from Catton Grove (Philadelphia Lane) along Angel Road into the City (part of my 92 route!), then out along Thorpe Road and Yarmouth Road to 'The Griffin' public house. Bingo! The gap between 7 and 7B was a black hole no longer.

Ten years later, at Main Works, from the wallet of Lenny Leverett, the Engineers' Records Officer - and also landlord of Marlingford 'Bell', and an old United man - emerged a photograph before which the scales fell from my eyes in that stunning revelatory fashion unique to the unexpected discovery of a photograph: a photograph which, at a stroke, resolves an ancient problem, settles an interminable argument, or fulfils a long-cherished longing to know, to understand, to see - and clearly.

It was another Epiphany moment, comparable in impact to the discovery of that fleet number, but of a different nature. There was

PW 3332 (AA 232)

at Philadelphia Lane, on Service 7A. The young conductor was Stanley Palmer, who was to become as legendary a figure within the Company as Lenny himself, and who completed fifty years of service, many as Operating Foreman at Surrey Street bus station in Norwich, where - in the relative quietness of mid-evening - operations would often be conducted from the bar of 'The Lame Dog', nearby. ("Come and get me if the phone rings, boy.")

Only God could possibly have known that ten years after that camera shutter clicked, Jack Burton would be born, only a few paces from the route of the 7A; and that fifty years after the photograph was taken, Jack Burton would conduct the funeral of that young conductor. As for the driver staring from the cab, with cloth cap and a splendid black moustache (which, together, suggested a character from a D H Lawrence novel), that was Billy Hubbard, who - I was informed - used to chew twist and expectorate regularly through the cab window. If a new driver asked to know the way to Pilson Green

12. This is Lenny Leverett's photograph which in 1957 provided me with the indisputable evidence that 'the United' had preceded my beloved Eastern Counties in Norwich. Here you see driver Billy Hubbard and conductor Stanley Palmer with PW 3332 (AA 232) at Philadelphia Lane, Catton Grove. The AEC chassis had been lengthened by United, fitted first with the new United body you see here, and then with pneumatic tyres, but the sale of AA 232 in 1929 meant that this bus would never carry the Eastern Counties name.

13. The connection was more surely made with Lenny's picture of United's VF 8514 (A 71), a 1930 Leyland TD1, because this vehicle became Eastern Counties A 85 when the new company took over in 1931. It was one I was to know well until withdrawal in 1950, albeit with its new 1938 body, and I saw it in the scrapyard as late as 1954, as I shall describe later. In this 1930-31 picture at Thorpe St Andrew's Hospital, Lenny Leverett himself was the conductor, with Charlie Peek as his driver.

17

14. *After a drink at Norwich's oldest inn, the Adam and Eve, you could watch Norwich City play Brentford, see Tom Mix at the Cinema Palace in Magdalen Street - or study the United timetable and go for a motor trip.*

(for instance) someone would quip - 'Billy Hubbard has just come in from there - just follow the marks on the road!'

But all that lay in the future; or do I mean the past? Time is the ultimate mystery. For the moment, I was impressed that United plugged the gap between 7 and 7B. Any organisation that could do that must definitely have a great deal more to contribute to my quest for enlightenment, knowledge, and understanding. Here, at least, I was on the right track.

Grandfather Smith lived on the next road to my own. He was not my grandfather, but belonged to a friend; I rated him highly for his stories of olden times. In only one matter did I find it necessary to correct him: in talking about buses, he would insist on referring to the United, and in the present tense.... "You'd think the United would put on an extra bus on Saturdays...." "It's not United now, it's Eastern Counties," I would correct him, patiently, politely and repeatedly. If he heard, he only grunted, in the way of old men, and never amended his practice. To me, 1931 was in that scarcely imaginable era Before Jack. Yet in 1946 it was only fifteen years distant - as yesterday to someone in his mid-eighties - a phenomenon to which I myself can now relate, utterly.

Apparently, this United had its bus station in Recorder Road, not far from where I lived. I looked - but couldn't pick up any bus vibrations from a street which, frankly, I didn't like and to which I couldn't (and still do not) relate. It was only far into adulthood that I was shown the few known surviving photographs which help to authentically stamp 'buses' on Recorder Road. It's a pity they are so tantalisingly few.

Yet, conversely, I had a childhood experience of a totally different nature, the significance of which became apparent only a few years ago. As a small boy, I trailed behind my mother each Saturday (around dinner-time, or during the afternoon), to Magdalen Street to shop. We passed the Lollards Pit, where martyrs were burned at the stake (including the saintly Thomas Bilney on another Saturday, in August 1531), then crossed the mediaeval Bishop's Bridge. I noted 'The Evening Gun', 'The King's Arms', 'The Bishop Bridge Tavern', 'The Red Lion', 'The Marquis of Granby', and 'The Adam and Eve' (which - in old photographs - displays a United timetable case). We passed St Helen's Church and the ancient Great Hospital, the Tabernacle (where John Wesley preached), then read the plaque in the wall which stated 'Near this place was killed Lord Sheffield in Kett's Rebellion

15. *Now there's a real coach! The Norwich civic coach delivers its passengers to the new Crown Court, on the site of the former gasworks. Among the trees in the left background is the Adam and Eve, and one minute's walk to the right is Fishergate. Standing left to right in front of the coach on Wednesday 8th June 1988 are the High Sheriff of Norfolk, Mr Justice Garland, the Sheriff of Norwich and Mrs Molly Burton.*

1st August 1549' - (the building is demolished, but the plaque was re-erected on the opposite side of the road). We stared at the Gas Works - now replaced by the Law Courts. How could a child know that, where the gatehouse and weighbridge could be seen, he would pass in the Civic Coach as Sheriff of Norwich, escorting the visiting red judge to what in those days would have been called the opening of the Assizes (but held at a more ancient venue, elsewhere).

Crossing the river again at Whitefriars Bridge - rebuilt in 1924, but with a tall lantern on each side, powerfully evocative, on misty days, of earlier times - we turned left into Fishergate. This was a 20-25 minute adult walk. As a child, I found it very long (going back was worse: it was uphill). But in Fishergate was a large open garage where corporation dustcarts were housed. It was beside St Edmund's church, on the corner of a little lane. From the entrance, I would peer into the gloom. It felt as if there ought to be a bus there. I *willed* a bus to be there - just one, right at the back - one I had overlooked at first. There never was; only dustcarts. Another misleading clue! I always looked - with the same expectation. I was always disappointed.

We continued to Woolworth's - about twenty paces from where I have lived for forty years, and where I am assembling these present reflections. How I would have marvelled if somebody had pointed at this house and said "That's where you will live when you are grown up"!

Another vivid recollection from those days in the mid 1940s is of cattle being driven through Magdalen Street from the cattle market on Norwich Hill, the bull being led by the ring in its nose. We sheltered in doorways. Those beasts looked big.

The postscript to this abiding memory came comparatively recently when I discovered - with an almost physical jolt - that United buses *had*, in fact, used that particular garage in Fishergate for a short period in the 1920s. I have no recollection whatsoever of anybody imparting that information to me as a child. I'm confident nobody did so. Like so many of our experiences, I think I *knew* - but that knowledge was hidden beneath the surface of my developing conscious mind, and lacked any tiny shred of material evidence to make possible the connection.

Perhaps it was just a guess, a hope, a lively imagination crowned by coincidence? Others will relate similar experiences which led nowhere! Yet most thoughtful people can remember occasions when, looking back, they realise that they knew.... that something teetered on the very brink of entering their consciousness as fact and knowledge. If our race lasts long enough, we shall learn to live at this deep level of awareness - indeed, we shall take it for granted in the way we have assimilated already the wonders of digital technology.

And, in my mind's eye, I can still see that little blond boy staring hard, longingly, searchingly, into the dustcart depot in Fishergate, for something he felt sure was there, somewhere - while his mother waited impatiently to reach Woolworth's. Sadly and reluctantly he came away. Decades of not-knowing lay ahead; but he would be vindicated.

I liked Woolworth's, especially the stationery counter. They sold neat little red note-books for tuppence, which slipped perfectly into the top pocket of a jacket. I'm holding one in my hand, even as I write. Energy and reassurance flow from it. Those note-books were ideal for copying runes, side numbers, route numbers, destination board details, railway engine numbers, names of ships visiting the Port of Norwich, and all those other important facts and particulars without which no man shall find wisdom. There was a larger version (perhaps for slightly older boys) which fitted comfortably into an inside pocket. One of mine survives, minus its cover; it is packed with the most amazing revelations.

There were also little pocket-sized note-pads available at Woolworth's - ones held together with a thin curly metal binder and (usually) with a Scottish terrier on the cover. These were good for writing out numbers from 1 - 999 and adding fleet and registration numbers as appropriate. However, this excellent scheme could only present a snapshot picture, accurate at a specific moment in time. It couldn't cope easily with rebodied, renumbered, withdrawn, or reclassified vehicles, which demanded more than one line. The present-day shapes of my letters and numerals remain those I learnt or adopted from registration plates, destination boards, and timetables.

In the days before the private car held universal sway, thousands travelled to the coast by train and by bus on bank holidays. Cromer (via Aylsham) was our usual destination, so I became familiar, at an early age, with what still remained what United had designated it: the Number Ten.

Four diverse memories survive. I recall going through the village of St Faiths and noting the workshop, beside the road, of Walter Woodcock, the thatcher and chapel stalwart - a man I was later to know and to admire greatly. I remember, too, an old country couple boarding a crowded double-decker - at Hanworth, or possibly Roughton - with an oval bath-tub of miscellaneous, junk-like items they wanted to take to Cromer. It was deposited - with much heaving and puffing - on the open platform, to the consternation of the conductor, who protested vigorously but eventually relented.

On some return journeys, I remember 'through passengers' for Norwich sometimes being loaded on to single-decker reliefs, which were then operated non-stop and without a conductor. On one such trip, my catch of small crabs escaped and caused surprise and alarm as they scurried about, to the annoyance and embarrassment of my mother.

My Aunt Audrey - in every other respect an admirable woman - caused disbelief, dismay, and embarrassment when I discovered she was afraid (and refused, point-blank) to travel on buses in case they tipped over. This incomprehensible attitude grieved me; I felt it brought dishonour on the family name. It has taken more than sixty years for me to stumble across a possible explanation of this phobia. A recent review of my papers produced an insight I had never previously considered. It was the result of placing four events in sequence.

13th May 1944 - A double-decker on Service 7 overturned while overtaking a line of bren-gun carriers, between Caister and Filby. A woman passenger was killed.

13th October 1944 - VG 4821 (AH 223) overturned at the junction of Market Street and Sidney Street in Cambridge.

17th April 1945 - A fully-loaded double-decker on Service 35 travelling between Hunstanton and King's Lynn mounted the verge at Babingley, fell into a ditch, and rolled on to a tree. Three passengers were killed.

16. *In the post-war period, crowds flocked to the coast by public transport on bank holidays. Our 22-mile journeys northward to Cromer are vividly evoked by this view of a packed NG 2721 (AH 186) waiting to depart from Norwich bus station on Service 10. The occasion was Whit Monday 17th May 1948, and crowds of intending passengers were waiting anxiously for a relief car to emerge from the garage. NG 2721 was a 1932 Leyland TD2 which had been rebodied in 1940 and was to run until 1950. (A B Cross)*

17. *This was the scene at the Babingley tragedy on the Sandringham royal estate on 17th April 1945. Photographic clues to the vehicle's identity are characteristically tantalising.*

29th August 1945 - A single-decker skidded and overturned on Eaton Hill. The conductress, Amy Mayes, of Blickling Hall Farm, was killed.

Suddenly, I thought of Aunt Audrey. Were these the events which, together, created her dread? It seems likely.

I discovered early that the Christmas and Easter fairs held on Norwich Hill, under the castle - when the pens of the cattle market would be removed for a week - were wonderful occasions for discovering very old buses enjoying an extended lease of life in the ownership of travelling showmen. Numbers were noted, but only if the acquisition was recent, or the showman's paint applied very thinly, was any form of identification possible. I must have seen some rare and early relics - but at such a tender age, and with nobody to guide me, the value and the depth of meaning of the experiences passed me by. Here, again, is a hauntingly moving image of a small child, amid the noise of generators and fair-ground music, flashing lights and eager showmen, candy-floss and happy crowds, staring behind the scenes, taking notes, searching for meaning.

How clearly I recall an unusual-looking single-decker parked in Bell Avenue! (The site is covered by a shopping mall, yet I could take you to within yards of the very spot.) The old bus had an Eastern Counties badge on the radiator and a registration number beginning UU. The date could well have been Easter 1947, towards the end of that very hard winter. This particular memory illustrates both the strength and the weakness of an inquisitive and intelligent child. I spotted the radiator badge, and observed the registration number. But because the letters were unfamiliar to me, and certainly not an East Anglian registration (like CL, VG, AH, PW, VF, NG, DX, EX, ER, VE, or FL), and because they had not appeared (to the best of my recollection) on any Eastern Counties bus I had ever seen in operation, I failed to make the connection.

I concluded that this could not be a genuine ex-Eastern Counties vehicle. The radiator must have been changed, or the badge added, or some equally confusing circumstance must have occurred. It took me a little time to reach this conclusion; some evidence pointed the other way; the bodywork *could* have been Eastern Coach Works; but you couldn't argue with a registration number.

It didn't occur to me that the runes which seemed a million miles from AAH were not utterly dissimilar to others in the Eastern Counties fleet with which I was entirely familiar (and which - like the AAHs - also carried AH side numbers). Why didn't the runes

UL 5354 (AH 230)
UL 5355 (AH 216)
UL 5356 (AH 231)

flicker across my mind? If UL, why not UU? I was faced with a set of conflicting facts which my childhood inexperience and lack of information had not yet equipped me to deal with in a logical, systematic, analytical manner. As I stared at the front of that strange-looking old bus, the facts simply didn't add up: and I didn't know what to do about it. The badge and the bodywork clashed with the registration number and the ugliness. Therefore, both could not be true. (It would be a decade before the concept of 'paradox' was explained to me.)

The possibility that other factors might exist of which I was as yet unaware, and the possibility that the world might be bigger than I perceived, had not yet penetrated deeply into my consciousness. I was quick to observe - but not always capable of interpreting and evaluating those observations. But I was not far away. And I never forgot. And, again, eventually light was given. It took several years, and I was well into adolescence before I discovered the significance of my observations at the fair. It took *many* more before I forgave myself for not preserving a permanent record. But I was very young, with no authority to consult on these matters.

For the record, however, there are strong reasons to conclude that the vehicle I saw was

UU 5148 (DE 9)

which had been acquired from Westminster Coaching Services in 1933, rebodied by Eastern Counties the following year, spent much of its working life at Cromer, and was withdrawn from service in 1945. It passed to a showman and was recorded at Great Yarmouth in April 1947. The travelling Easter fair at Norwich moved on, next, to Great Yarmouth.

18. *The solution to the puzzle of the old Eastern Counties bus which I saw with a showman at the fair! This photograph was taken at Cromer bus station ten years earlier. In time-honoured manner, the bright young thing is thoughtlessly obliterating the registration number-plate, but the fleet number DE 9 tells us that we are looking at Dennis 32-seater UU 5148.*

19. *In a 1937 scene, again at Cromer bus station, sister vehicle YX 1491 (DE 6) also had the registration plate obscured but the fleet number visible. The men in uniform, all with caps, collars and ties and clean black shoes, and the bus with its smooth flowing lines, smart livery and gentle advertising, are a credit to the company. Attention to detail created a harmonious whole, and we are the poorer for its passing. (H H Tansley, Photographer)*

I referred, earlier, to

XV 3774 (AH 227)

- which points to the significant place the number retains in my memory. I recall going fishing (with net, for minnows, dace, gudgeon, loach, and bullheads) at Costessey Mill (Service 13A) with a friend, one sunny morning. We returned at dinner-time, which was unusual; normally, we stayed until late afternoon.

Two mental pictures from that day have never faded. Firstly, I can see the light and shade of the sunlight shining through the trees beside the churchyard of St Walstan's RC Church, at Costessey. Why has this image survived? Maybe because the unusual time of our departure meant that the sunshine lit the scene from an unfamiliar angle; it was comforting, reassuring, appealing, and good. I've looked again at this precious picture many times over the years, and it has never lost its potency and attractiveness.

Secondly, I can remember, back in Thorpe Station yard, standing in front of the bus, (much like Alan Strang, who 'worshipped' horses in Peter Schaffer's *Equus*), looking up at the registration plate and reading XV 3774, feeling the heat of the silent resting vehicle, smelling its diesel and its warmth, and revelling in the nearness of this god. Wearing short trousers, I 'worshipped' with a fishing net in one hand and a paint-tin full of tiddlers in the other. The experience was, at once, sensual and spiritual. But I knew nothing of the vehicle's story; and if I had been told, I would have struggled to comprehend and master the information. My instincts and emotions were more alert and advanced than my intellectual development.

I knew it had two sisters, XV 3775 and XV 3776; but several years would pass before I would understand that it began life as a 1928 Dodson-bodied coach, operated by Palanquin Coaches of London W3. It passed to Varsity Coaches Limited, Cambridge, in June 1930, which was acquired by Eastern Counties in August 1933. Numbered AT 139, it was fitted with a new Eastern Counties highbridge double-decked body in August 1934, painted in the livery of Norwich Electric Tramways (see later), and fitted with destination blinds. It was numbered 48. It returned to the main Eastern Counties fleet in December 1935 (and obtained destination boards and red livery). XV 3774 was scrapped in September 1949.

How I would love to have gazed on that number plate again, when all its rich meaning had been revealed! But, by then, it had long disappeared. Yet still I see it, clearly, in my mind's eye.

Some strange vehicles with full, rounded fronts appeared in 1949. I didn't like them at all - the lines, the shape didn't appeal. The CBs were Beadle / Bedford chassisless vehicles, and were followed the next year by another new class - the CDs - which were Eastern Coach Works / Dennis chassisless creations, and looked even stranger.

One wet afternoon I was at Rosary Corner, in Norwich, when a CB went past on Service 7B to Panxworth. I was astonished! The tyres on the wet road seemed to be singing their destination. It was perfect onomatopoeia centred on the 'nx'. What ridiculous, trivial items stick in the mind of a child, and are never erased. But my ear was nearer the road than adult ears. Say 'Panxworth' properly, with a lingering 'nx', and you will hear the squelch of wet tyres on Thorpe Road as a 1949 CB passes Rosary Corner on 7B.

The Main Workshops at Cremorne Lane, sited behind Head Office and alongside the railway line to Great Yarmouth, were not very far from my house and became an irresistible magnet. In summer, the great doors of the body shop were sometimes rolled aside to reveal an inviting world of timber, sheet-metal, paint, upholstery and buses in various stages of overhaul and repair.

I particularly liked peering through the little wicket-door next to the dock, to glimpse the secret world inside. I recall, especially, the atmosphere of late afternoons in winter, when outside it was dark, but inside was wonderland: lights, shadows, oil; buses propped up on trestles (with axles missing); buses delicensed, new buses, buses for scrap; accident-damaged buses; skilled fitters working at lathes, overhauling units, testing engines, repairing gearboxes; chassis, mysterious buses, buses awaiting collection. The spell was powerful; the warm, welcoming smell part of the thrill. Then a chargehand would shout, and we would be gone. Today, a housing development covers the site.

20. This is definitely one for the connoisseur! Buses were diverted around the ancient Guildhall in Norwich on 7th November 1936 while tramlines were being removed. The bus on the left, irritatingly obscured by the pole which was not only a lamp post but had also served to support the tramway overhead, looks like one of the six rebodied ex-Varsity coaches - so it could even be XV 3774! In the background at the top of the hill is what appears to be either LG 16 or 17 which, new in June that year, carried the bodies from DL 1 and 2. (Eastern Daily Press)

21. With this picture you see why the 1949 Beadle-Bedfords did not appeal to me, with their stark, ungainly lines, and narrow wheel track. This one was HPW 812 (CB 827), sitting in Surrey Street garage, Norwich, after a trip on Service 5A. Behind, ENG 349 (LL 599) was ready for a 'special' run to the institution for the elderly and infirm at Shipmeadow, beyond Bungay. (Omnibus Society / C F Klapper)

Sometimes, as a child, I organised and operated my own bus service. From the lamp-post in our alley, I planned routes in different directions, urging and encouraging friends to operate them with me. This game aimed to provide a regular frequency, and it was important to observe every stop - not least, to regain breath. Sound effects were expected, and manual gestures - steering wheel, gear stick, hand signals - were compulsory. How strange we must have looked, running down the road. I couldn't help noticing that the friends I cajoled into playing this game always got back to the bus station lamp-post before me, and though I said nothing, secretly I sometimes suspected them of operating 'shorts'. Then, again - none of us had watches, so perhaps they were just running early.

22. This picture of the rebodied DX 8424 (AH 149) at Thunder Lane (Ring Road) on Service 82 circa 1948 illustrates the route on which the Sign of the Clean Nappy was given. It also introduces us to the Eastern Counties Road Car Company - 'the Road Car', to whom this Leyland TD1 was new in 1930. As I shall mention later, Road Car preceded the 1931 new Eastern Counties Omnibus Company Ltd in Suffolk.

Back in the real (?!) world, Service 90 - out along Newmarket Road to Cringleford - was operated by saloons during the week, but by double-deckers on Sundays. I recall being on the top-deck, travelling towards the city. Somewhere near the Girls' High School, as I was writing important details in my note-book (listing the bus stops, perhaps) I happened to remark that it was difficult to write neatly when the bus was in motion. Immediately, my mother remarked: "You won't make a very good bus conductor if you can't write when the bus is moving!" I realised instantly that, in modern parlance, I had scored an own goal. My confusion and mortification were intense. I can still remember feeling: "I wish I hadn't said that". I felt it had been a serious tactical error, and I couldn't recall ever feeling quite like that before. I have, however, had the experience many times, since.

A similar occasion provided an insight even more profound (though some may find its inclusion here unseemly). As the family alighted from the Service 82 at Riverside Road it was found, to our dismay, that the youngest member and the bus seat were both smeared liberally with excrement. The child was scolded severely and the situation reported to the conductor, whom I recall as being less than gracious in his understanding. We left the vehicle in disgrace and climbed the steep St Matthew's Road wearily, the baby puzzled by the cloud which had descended over the brightness of our day.

Arriving home, the baby was laid on the floor (probably on old newspapers) and the offending garments removed gingerly. Then came the revelation. When the big safety-pin was unfastened, the nappy was found to be unsoiled! We stared in great surprise. When the implications became clear, we were filled with remorse and indignation. The child was blameless. Whoever applied the nappy and pin was blameless. The mess had been left by another. Our baby had been deposited in it.

The child kicked and laughed as it lay on the floor, glad to be freed from its pungent prison, happy to be restored to the family's favour, and relishing the sympathy and affection now lavished guiltily upon it. I never forgot The Sign of the Clean Nappy, which followed our humiliation on Service 82. I may have lacked theological understanding, but I felt sure this great wonder contained an important lesson - which, of course, it did. Putting aside the vexed question of original sin, many would agree (whatever the terminology) that we are born into a 'fallen' creation, marred by human selfishness. Or - to put it another way - we are dropped in it.

The front seats of the upper saloon were the most coveted by children, but if compelled to travel downstairs, the favourite seat was the near-side front, staring out beneath the canopy. The driver, in his cab,

23. A rare glimpse of a bus from Mile Cross at the Duke Street terminus, about to reverse into the yard of The Duke's Palace. The view is from St John Maddermarket; the traffic policeman stands at Charing Cross. However poor the photographic quality, the discovery of such a picture as evidence of things long gone is a moment of high joy for an enthusiast. (George Plunkett)

was to the right, the radiator cap and the bonnet were in the centre, and the huge, satisfying near-side wing on the left. These veered, as one, to left or right in response to the movement of the steering wheel, itself an object of particular veneration.

3. Good taste and high quality

Sometimes a friendly conductor could be persuaded to donate an unused ticket roll or, at least, a generous portion of one part-used. Here was treasure indeed. On these I could record many important matters, carefully rolling up the reel behind me, as I went, until the effect resembled a miniature scroll of Jewish scriptures. Memories are remarkable for their arbitrary nature: I recall distinctly writing 'DUKE ST' on a ticket roll in this fashion. Duke Street was the city terminus of what I knew as Service 86/87 - the first route in Norwich to be created for tram replacement.

This was another thick strand of adult reminiscence which, as an inquisitive child, I couldn't afford to ignore - for its relevance to my nameless quest, my longing and my perpetual delight, was plain: the trams.

I can't remember how I learned what the word 'tram' meant. There were no great systems within a hundred miles. Norwich Electric Tramways Company had ceased operations on 10th December 1935. I'd missed the trams by three years and ten months - a fact which still touches a raw nerve and ignites a quiet burning resentment (seldom put into words before but which, suddenly, I realise I have never dealt with entirely). I was baptised on 10th December 1939.

How the concept registered, I cannot say; but register it did - in the most compelling manner. I found a photograph on the wall, at one of the Norwich museums. Like a lover, I wanted to possess this image - to be able to produce it, and stare at it: so I drew it. After all these years I still find moving this scene of the small child drawing the objects of his affection and commitment. It was not only the trams. I struggled also to capture the beautiful lines of the AHs rebodied in the 1930s, and the near perfection of the later LJs. My efforts brought little satisfaction.

We were poor. Any photographs I saw were only few, and taken by other people. The world of modern photography was as far from our imagining as the moon, physically, or the time of Christ, chronologically. I improved slightly. Eventually, I could draw a representation of a 3ft 6in gauge, open-topped tramcar with commendable accuracy; but it was all in the mind.... How I longed to touch, and to see!

My first photograph of a Norwich tram was a cutting from the *Eastern Evening News*, which gave me almost more joy than any other acquisition in my entire lifetime. This was followed by others from the same source. Letters to the editor and occasional articles frequently attracted wide interest and an enthusiastic response, which would then produce a fresh selection of (sometimes contradictory) letters. All those details I noted and compared with the oral evidence I had taken, particularly from my step-father, who had been born in 1902 - just two years after the system opened. From him I obtained knowledge of the routes and the route colours.

However, I was well into my teens before the photographs taken by M J O'Connor came into my possession. They created an impression very similar to that of seeing AA 232 at Philadelphia Lane on Service 7A. I saw nothing I didn't already know - but I saw it more clearly than ever before, and from different angles, and in different locations. The word was made, if not flesh then certainly paper, ink, and wondrous image. But this past, too, lay still in the future.

Physical evidence of the trams' existence was sparse - though there must have been more, if only I had been pointed in the right direction. There were splendid poles with long bracket-arms in Magpie Road and Queens Road, which once supported the overhead wires. There was a section of track in Thorpe Station yard which had provided a link out of the station on to the Riverside Road and Mousehold Heath stretch of track, from which an extension had been constructed in the First World War to the factory of Boulton and Paul, where aircraft were built.

The tram shed survived, used by a wholesale grocer, with some track still visible in front, and with the offices beside. The thought of the hours of silent worship I would gladly have offered on this spot, but had been denied, weighed heavily; and I am still sad that I was in my twenties before I heard about, and photographed, the fast-deteriorating hulk of car 8, in use as an allotment shed at Denmark Opening, just a hundred yards from the depot doors. I simply never met the people who could have told me.

Car 40 was in much better condition at Hellesdon, in use as a garden shed. The kindly householder even permitted access, as into the holy of holies. It was later still (when employed as a driver myself) that, driving on Service 18, I arrived in Hempnall and noticed a disused chicken-shed behind a hedge. The bus stopped, the crew investigated: a Norwich tram, in its death-throes! I can remember wanting to stay, even amid the squalor, to pay appropriate last respects.... But time pressed.... we were due at Fritton 'Three Nags'.

As I thought about the trams, it occurred to me that some Eastern Counties bus routes seemed, clearly, to be based on former tram routes. Anyhow, the child to whom the runes AAH 136 - AAH 145 meant more than the word 'father' - my parents had separated early in the war, and I had established my relationship with the TD4s long before mother remarried - continued to observe, and listen, and grow in understanding.

24. *The Norwich Electric Tramways Company commenced operation in 1900, and its fleet never progressed beyond the initial design of open-top four-wheel double-deckers, despite the purchase of many new cars in the 1920s. In consequence, by the end of that decade they were no match for the rapidly developing motor-buses which took their place. This fine view of car 21 from the camera of the legendary Maurice O'Connor was taken at the end of Riverside Road opposite the entrance to Thorpe station, when the tram was more than thirty years old. (National Tramway Museum)*

25. *When I found and photographed the remains of original five-bay car 8 in 1963, it had been used as an allotment shed at Denmark Opening since being replaced by a new car in 1925. The new No. 8 was different - it had four rectangular side windows with separate opening lights above.*

I knew 'the United' was part of the story, even if the true nature of that involvement had yet to be revealed. If only a VF-registered vehicle had operated on the Newcastle-Lowestoft service (which United Automobile Services Ltd, of Grange Road, Darlington, A T Evans General Manager, insisted on calling Service 50, but which was really Service S, because Service 50 went from Great Yarmouth to Ipswich) then my senses would have been put on alert, my mind into overdrive, and I might - just might - have been driven to ask the right questions (if I could have found the right person to ask).

But the Norfolk 'United' pre-1931 (I can't even remember how I learned that date) was part of my heritage. 7A proved it. And the trams, likewise. (I'm still not sure about their livery: some told me chocolate brown, some said maroon - it must have been one of those slightly unusual shades people find hard to describe, particularly when it weathers.) I even obtained a tram ticket. I bought a second-hand book in Elm Hill, and found someone had used it as a book-marker. I'm tormented, now, by the dread that it might actually have been issued on a Tramways bus.

Surprisingly, it was only a few years ago that I was taught where to look for surviving wall hooks and rosettes which had supported the tram wires in the walls of old buildings in the city. Several still survive - and one lamp post. So - Eastern Counties Omnibus Company Limited, 79, Thorpe Road, Norwich; the United (but not of Grange Road, Darlington); Norwich Electric Tramways Company: the picture was taking shape. Plenty to work on there as I continued writing the magic runes in my 2d note-books from Woolworth's. But then the grown-ups threw another spanner in the works - as, of course, grown-ups always do. They started talking about the Tramways Buses. It was some time before I could set this concept in context, but gradually, I grasped the basic situation.

Tramways Buses were painted in the same indeterminate livery as the trams and were owned by the Norwich Electric Tramways Company. Their depot was the big garage at Ladysmith Road, Silver Road, behind the tram sheds. I knew nothing of this building's history. It never occurred to me that it *had* a history. Eastern Counties used this large garage for storing. It was packed with delicensed coaches in the winter. Here, exciting views of new, delicensed, damaged, or withdrawn vehicles could be obtained by staring through holes in the corrugated iron walls where bolts and rivets had dropped out. It was locked and unattended. There was no other way. The newish-looking house beside this garage was built, I was told, for the garage foreman. Its unique garden fence was made of discarded tram trolley-standards.

Imagine the excitement when I peered through a rivet-hole one day and saw a green double-decker. It turned out to be

ARR 831 (KD 28)

purchased with the business of Clarke's of Felixstowe and never put into Eastern Counties livery. It had originally entered service with West Bridgford UDC; its next destination, alas, was the scrapyard.

Tramways Buses were used a) for tram replacement on Aylsham Road (1925), b) for feeder-services from tram termini to the council estates that were springing up on the edge of the city (in a massive slum clearance programme), c) to open up new routes.

In fact, it had been Tramways Buses which first operated up my very own road! If ever I have emulated St Thomas, this was the claim that drove me to it. Tramways buses going past (what would be) my birthplace? Not red buses but buses of a colour nobody seemed able to agree upon? Not Eastern Counties, not even the United - but Tramways Buses!? This time, the light dawned very slowly indeed. I found it difficult to visualise anything different operating regularly on Service 92. (I presumed - wrongly - that that would have been the service number, because that was the number which had *always* operated up Marion Road - well, certainly since 1939; it was one of those fixed facts that couldn't be challenged or questioned).

At the end of the war, the TD4s which operated on Marion Road were augmented increasingly by 'the new buses': i.e. Bristol K types, with roller blinds, including one on the near side, above the platform - a practice soon abandoned. (A few, originally, had wooden slatted seats). The blinds were a great novelty: Eastern Counties buses usually displayed the distinctive horizontally-hinged clicker-board indicators which marked them out from all other operators I had encountered, and which I regarded as works of art. (One hangs on my study wall.) They were so called because when one was

26. So this *was one of the mysterious Tramways Buses! At Mile Cross in about 1928, driver Arthur Spurgeon and conductor Reggie Brookes were ready to leave for Duke Street with one of the four open-topped Short Bros-bodied Guy BXs (CL 9123-6, nos 9-12) which had been new in December 1926. At this stage they were not noticeably more advanced than the trams, except perhaps for upholstered seats.*

27. *On the other hand, 1929 Leyland TD1 demonstrator TE 9855 was a real head-turner. It led to Norwich Tramways subsequently purchasing ten Leyland double-deckers, although after demonstration duties this one passed to Bury Corporation. It was photographed at the Silver Road bus garage, and twenty years later it was through these walls that I squinted to see what was inside.*

attached to the bus, it clicked into place behind suitable spring fasteners. The lettering was black on cream; county route numbers were painted red.

But back to the Tramways Buses! Apart from the TD4s (AHs) and new Bristols (LKHs), only the lunchtime Bristol single-decker workers' reliefs (LLs) with runes beginning CNG, CVF, EAH, or ENG, had ever ventured here. I would need a photograph. Without a photograph, I would not believe.

But our road was not of the kind which attracted photographers. And should it ever have done so, they would surely have waited for the intrusive bus to pass before allowing it to occupy so large a part of the scene they wished to record. So the picture eluded me - until 2002. Norwich City FC celebrated its centenary, and a special exhibition was mounted at the Castle Museum. It included a splendid aerial photograph of the club's former ground, which was situated at the top of our road. I ignored the pitch and players, and stared in amazement at the top of the picture. Even old men can have Epiphany moments. Descending St Leonard's Road and about to turn left into the road where I would be born a few years later (when - red or grey - TD4s would reign unchallenged) was a Leyland TD2 in the livery of Norwich Electric Tramways Company. I could have wept.

My father-in-law, who died in 2002, lives on in my memory as a lively and irrepressible nonagenarian. Occasionally, he would exclaim, à propos of nothing in particular: "Good taste and high quality in its literary and artistic work are the keynotes of Punch!" Born in 1905, he lived as a boy in the village of Horsford, and travelled to Norwich regularly each Saturday on the carrier's cart from Brandiston, putting up at 'The Duke's Palace' (later, the city terminus of the Aylsham Road buses) and helping to deliver parcels.

On one occasion, towards the end of the First World War, he was asked to bring a parcel to Norwich urgently. He walked from Horsford to the Aylsham Road tram terminus at Vicarage Road, then caught a tram into the city, by that wonderfully circuitous route through old Norwich which made it an obvious candidate for conversion to bus operation. (I am still searching for photographs of trams in Oak Street and Sussex Street.)

Facing a young Charles Stanley Hutchison as he clutched the precious parcel was an advertisement for a famous magazine. He learnt it by heart on that journey, never forgot it, and was glad to recite it eighty years later. Many might feel that good taste and high quality are but two of the values which characterised, at its best, the age of the tram.

The image of an even younger Stanley squeezed aboard the carrier's cart is appealing. As a bus driver, it always gave me pleasure to remember that I stood in a long line of waggoners, carriers, coachmen, and tramwaymen stretching back over the centuries. Sometimes, in the cab, I would sing the old West Country folk-song, *The Jolly Waggoner*:

> Sing 'Whoa!' my lads, sing 'Whoa!'
> Drive on, my lads, heigh ho!
> Who would not lead the stirring life
> We jolly waggoners do?

4. A great and wondrous sign

The girl who lived two doors from me had relatives in Liverpool whom she visited with her family, every summer. I fantasised each year, that - at the last moment - they would unexpectedly (and irrationally) invite me to go with them. I knew there were trams in Liverpool, and longed to see them. (Had I known the beauty of the Green Goddess, I might even have resorted to prayer for my neighbours to receive enlightenment and right guidance in this matter. But prayer lay in the future.) The girl who lived six doors down went to Bournemouth! I knew there were trolleybuses in Bournemouth.... but, at least, (entering my teens), I was able to visit Ipswich and see them there - including some wonderfully primitive-looking single-deckers. I little knew that, one day, I would live on the route of the last tram-to-trolleybus conversion in Britain; (and, please note, I did not say *England*....).

So the gift, the fascination, the exploration continued as the small boy grew slightly bigger. Other things mattered to him also: natural history was a source of inspiration and wonderment from the

28. *Just for once, never mind the football, look at the bus! A Norwich Tramways Leyland TD2, new in September 1932, descends St Leonard's Road on its winding route through Thorpe Hamlet on Service 3 to Lakenham. Within seconds it will turn left into Marion Road, visible on the right. The Nest was the home of Norwich City, and the last game there was played on 6th May 1935.*

29. *This lovely picture postcard captures the charm of a bygone age - try to imagine modern motor traffic at the same spot! In this tramway scene, car 10 passes Eade Road as it travels along Aylsham Road towards the city. On board, one young boy could have been staring at the advertisements....*

AYLSHAM ROAD. NORWICH.

outset: kingfisher, stickleback, kingcup. History was vital, too: Boadicea, Romans, Angles, Danes. Coins, stars, stamps - all were interesting, all seemed to unlock doors to greater understanding and other, fuller worlds. But underpinning them all was the obsession, or love-affair, with the omnibus - particularly those belonging to Eastern Counties Omnibus Company Limited, 79, Thorpe Road, Norwich. (I wanted to love trams, too - all the willpower was there: but no opportunity had yet presented itself, one hundred miles east of anywhere.)

Like most love-affairs, this one glowed with a varied intensity. Life would be impossible if its most vivid manifestations represented its constant state. There were periods when the commitment and interest glowed quietly and contentedly - watching and enjoying, but with no compulsion to undertake fevered activity. At other times, I couldn't wait for the dinner-bell so I could spend half-an-hour on the traffic island outside Thorpe Station noting details of every vehicle in one of the tuppenny books from Woolworth's. Another favourite venue at these times of intensity was, of course, the Bus Station, immediately after tea, watching the buses running in and queuing impatiently to get on the pumps. Naturally, these included some of the TD4s, displaying '92 BUS STATION' boards.

To me, it is self-evident that through this 'hobby' - a word which never seems to be adequate - a variety of worthwhile incidental benefits were accruing, educational and emotional. I learnt to write quickly and accurately; the routes taught me the geography of East Anglia; the smell of hot tyres and diesel became my incense; I learnt to distinguish shapes, and view them aesthetically: those LJ coaches of 1936-37 I found moving in their beauty of line; I learnt to ask questions, be polite, show respect, and say thank you; my powers of observation were honed, and my historical perspective was reinforced.

My analytical and forensic skills developed as I wrestled with Eastern Counties, the United, United Automobile Services Limited Grange Road Darlington, Norwich Electric Tramways Company, the Tramways Buses, and an increasing - apparently endless - range of titles and topics, ancient and modern, such as Great Yarmouth Corporation, Lowestoft Corporation, North Western (who were they? and where was Charles Street, Stockport?), Trent, (whose coaches seemed more numerous than Eastern Counties at weekends), and Metropolitan Coaches of Great Yarmouth, some of whose oncoming Dennis and Bedford coaches (I noticed, suddenly, cycling through Blofield one morning on the way to Great Yarmouth) had mysteriously acquired Eastern Counties fleet numbers. What did it mean? What was relevant, and what was not? Where were the lines to be drawn?

None of this came from formal schooling. It began long before I trotted off to the half-of-a-school Hitler had missed two years earlier. It came from within. So it came from God. Why? For my own exploration into God, maybe? For a sensitive awareness of the intricate and inter-dependent nature of the creation - for that is where God dwells - so that I might learn to apprehend and discern his hand, and his nature? To equip me, in some fashion, for life; or, perhaps, some special task; for the fulfilment of a destiny? To bring life abundant, and gladness, to others? All those question-cum-answers I believe, firmly and truly.

Nothing is meaningless or wasted in the economy of God. There is purpose in our passion. But, again, I don't know if I'm leaping backwards or forwards. For another Epiphany moment was at hand - more dramatic than both the discovery of fleet numbers (which, by now, I'd mastered thoroughly) and the photograph of AA 232 on 7A (which lay in the future).

In those post-war days we wandered miles in our play. Once, at mid-day, with the sun shining brightly, I recall vividly being on Mousehold, 184 acres of heathland which fringes the city on the north-east side. (The zig-zagging route of the 92 was to enable it, in effect, to climb up to the heath, though houses - like mine - had been built on its lower slopes.) The trams had ventured on to the heath, but only in summer-time. (In winter, they terminated at the Cavalry Barracks.) It was in the immediate vicinity of the tram terminus that a most amazing experience occurred - though, of course, fifteen years had elapsed since the last car had departed from the bandstand and the fountain.

There is no way of describing the following incident which will do justice to the immensity of its impact. With friends, I came through some trees and, emerging, saw a sight which astounded me as overwhelmingly as that granted to the children at Fatima. It was a bus - a brand-new, double-decker

30. Here is one of the 1936 Bristol JO5G 30-seat coaches whose graceful form so captured my imagination. Driver Bert Vurley, of whom more later, was helping passengers to alight from AVF 367 (LJ 447) in the late 1940s, on one of the Norwich - London services.

31. At first I was unable to understand why vehicles of Metropolitan Coaches of Great Yarmouth had acquired Eastern Counties fleet numbers. The dilemma is illustrated by these two Bedford OBs on excursions, KAH 954 (BS 954) on the right in standard red and cream coach livery, and EX 6700 (BS 923) on the left retaining the Metropolitan name and their chocolate and cream livery. ECOC had purchased the Metropolitan business in 1951. (A B Cross / J Higham collection)

bus - painted in the most gorgeous, exotic, livery. It had been brought on to the heath to be photographed officially, and stood proud and gleaming, against a background of gorse, heather, and birch.

This was the world turned upside down. Double-decker buses were not those colours. Intellectually, I was not sure I approved. But intellect can be overrated, and my heart leapt within me. O vision glorious! From the depths of my being I responded to this Epiphany moment of all Epiphany moments. I responded with an unuttered cry of approval and affirmation. This, surely, was what life was all about; for this moment had I been conceived.

What did it mean? We moved forward cautiously. I simply could not have been more spellbound if we had stumbled upon a spacecraft, or seen the beam of light which shone upon the broken body of young St William of Norwich, which was discovered thereabouts in 1144. Cream, green, and orange; and upon the side: GLASGOW CORPORATION.

I nearly swooned. There is only a certain amount of wonder a small boy can take. Glasgow! What romance was hid in the very word. "Glasgow belongs to me"! We listened to the wireless in those days, and knew (a little of) a far wider variety of music than most youngsters do, today. Glasgow - Scotland! This bus didn't even belong in England. Notices made plain that this gleaming new bodywork had been built here in Norwich by Mann Egerton. One of the boys I was with was later to serve his apprenticeship with that company (a name very well-known in East Anglia) before joining Eastern Counties as a bodybuilder.

The relevant pocket note-book from F W Woolworth has long-since gone the way of all flesh and most pocket note-books: but Mann Egerton built only a handful of double-decker bodies, and only one went to Glasgow Corporation. My vision, therefore, was of FYS 494, a Daimler which was exhibited at Earl's Court in 1950 before entering service as Glasgow D 66.

The odds against my enjoying this experience (which is still as vivid today as ever) were, upon reflection, astronomically long. A space of half-an-hour, on one particular day, in a precise location, some distance from my house, and where I would rarely be found at that time of day - and one vehicle only!

The impact on my imagination was enormous. Glasgow was a large city, I knew that. A great city, with the River Clyde, and shipyards and all kinds of heavy engineering. It sounded the opposite of everything I had grown up to know and recognise - the Norfolk Broads, wide open skies, hundreds of ancient parish churches. But Glasgow must be full of buses painted like this. What a sight! What a place it must be! Furthermore, I knew it had trams - hundreds of them. Were they, too, painted like this? The mind boggled.

Had that experience occurred to an enthusiast today, he would probably have found ways of acting upon it, travelling north promptly to see for himself. As it was, I was young, poor, and living in a heavily bombed but still attractive mediaeval city in a land jutting out into the North Sea miles from anywhere. No action was remotely possible. I could only dream.

However, looking back it is impossible not to see that experience on Mousehold Heath as an extraordinarily significant event. Before I could get to Glasgow, Glasgow came to me. But I was sure this was a journey I would make, eventually; that, one day, I would pursue the vision and follow this bus to what - with livery like that - must be surely the city of God, where buses and trams abounded, painted not red, nor blue, nor grey - but cream, green, and orange. One day! The coat of arms on the side of FYS 494 bore the motto: 'Let Glasgow flourish'. I didn't know, then, that the full version was: 'Let Glasgow flourish by the preaching of His Word and the praising of His Name'. It was more apt than I could have possibly foreseen.

I would have been intrigued to have learned that United's first two motor buses, supplied new in 1912, were Halley open-sided single-deckers

V 1501 (1)

V 1502 (2)

manufactured at Halley's works at Yoker, on the outskirts of Glasgow, the numbers being issued by Lanarkshire County Council.

32. *The Riverside Road tramway had a summer extension to the Fountain, Mousehold Heath, where car 14 was pictured. Just here, nearly fifty years later, the Vision on the Heath was given.*

33. *That glorious vision of 1950 was somewhat subdued by the time that the photograph below was taken in Renfrew Street, Glasgow, somewhere between 1955 and 1958. Nevertheless, this is it, FYS 494 (D 66) - a rare beast combining a Mann Egerton eight-feet-wide body and a standard 7'6" Daimler CVD6 chassis. The vivid orange, green and cream livery which made such an unforgettable impression loses more than most by being shown here in black and white - look at the trams on the back cover! (Jim Thomson)*

34. FNG 823 (LKH 61), a 1947 Bristol K type outside Thorpe Station on Service 80 to Harvey Lane (Morse Avenue). These Bristols were 'the new buses' which first augmented, then began to replace, the Leylands. (Maurice Doggett)

5. Making progress

Each year brought greater knowledge and greater confidence in the handling of my material. I was 11 in October 1950 and, no doubt, developing all the self-confidence of a small boy preparing to enter his teens.

I heard that Eastern Counties would lend a copy of the Fleet List to any interested inquirer. I availed myself of this facility, and duly received a copy of the sacred scriptures over which I pored tremblingly, copying, copying, copying. The loan of that Fleet List gave me my first authoritative overview of the Company's current vehicles. Together with a set of timetables, I was ready for anything. But the history-angle was a different kettle of fish: I knew there was still much work to be done to master matters which, inconsiderately, had been and gone before I arrived and had had time to supervise them.

The Eastern Counties fleet provided an unusually absorbing subject for study and amusement. Not only had the company been formed by the amalgamation of four companies, each with its own distinctive vehicle types; from the outset, other operators - large and small - had been taken over, and many of their vehicles added to the fleet. This meant standardising, as far as possible, the appearance of the vehicles in a common livery and - most notably- the addition of the distinctive destination boards.

Furthermore, a comprehensive re-bodying programme in the 1930s had extended the life (and altered the appearance) of many vehicles which had featured in the Company's original fleet in 1931. This left confused young enthusiasts studying photographs of two obviously different buses with the same runes. A second spell of rebodying, post-war, had also to be negotiated and understood.

For me, the renumbering of the fleet in December 1946 passed almost unnoticed, largely because my TD4s, most of the other A/AHs, and my second favourites - the LGs - were unaffected. Soon, I acquired a basic understanding of the thinking behind the fleet numbering system, which - as mentioned - ran from 1-999, each with a prefix of letters. A secret code seemed necessary to interpret

35. KNG 699 (LE 699), a 1950 dual-purpose Bristol L5G, had worked through to Middlesbrough where it was seen in Park Street on 29th July 1954. These vehicles possessed a profound attractiveness in their simplicity, which the passage of sixty years has not diminished. (D S Burnicle)

these fleet numbers, and I worked to crack it. I reached certain conclusions:

> A = Leyland
> B = Bedford
> D = Dennis
> L = Bristol
> P = Tilling-Stevens
> S = coach
> H = highbridge vehicle.

Sometimes, the second letter in a fleet number indicated the chassis type. For instance, the new standard double-deckers were designated LK/LKH, i.e. Bristol (L) 'K' type/Highbridge. These heralded the dawn of a new chapter which would last until the coming of the Lodekkas, nearly a decade later. They entered the fleet with a new brand of LL, whose fleet numbers continued in sequence from the earlier vehicles of that class but which again, were distinguishable immediately by their destination blinds. In both instances these modern vehicles were clearly superior to the old, and their details were all carefully noted: but their standardisation left me vaguely dissatisfied and uneasy, and my affection for the vehicles which bore the authentic and distinctive clicker-boards began, consciously, to intensify.

There were two particular exceptions. After LL 696 came seven vehicles of similar design but in semi-coach livery, and with comfortable coach seats. The appearance of these dual-purpose vehicles - LE class - I found profoundly satisfying. I noticed that United Automobile Services Limited Grange Road Darlington A T Evans General Manager also had some, but, for reasons beyond me, insisted on classifying them BBE. These runes remain very meaningful:

> KNG 697 (LE 697)
> KNG 698 (LE 698)
> KNG 699 (LE 699)
> KNG 700 (LE 700) - the roundness of the number made it
> specially significant.

KNG 701 (LE 701)

KNG 702 (LE 702)

KNG 703 (LE 703).

Before the LL sequence resumed, a run of coaches intervened, the likes of which I had never imagined operating for Eastern Counties - the curved, full-fronted, 'Queen Mary' coaches:

KNG 704 (LS 704) The Norwich City FC team coach.

KNG 705 (LS 705)

KNG 706 (LS 706)

KNG 707 (LS 707)

KNG 708 (LS 708).

For me these are runes which stir the heart, meaningfully and deeply.

When the eight-feet-wide double-deckers arrived I was transported to another plane. Never mind the lack of clicker-boards. Their beauty of proportion over-ruled all critical thoughts concerning standardisation. There simply could never be too many creatures of such grace and strength. Let the land be filled with 8 ft-wide LKHs! Sometimes, I saw them hurrying through Norwich, new from the coachworks at Lowestoft: LKHs heading north, in the same livery but called by some other name (BBH) with 'United' painted on the side, and 'Body by Eastern Coach Works' notices displayed in the windows. (Incidentally, I had no inkling that ECW was originally part of United, and that bodies built between 1931 and 1936 - including AH 232-241 - were Eastern Counties bodies.)

Our few wartime LKs and LKHs, with ungainly, angular bodies (but with clicker-boards) disappeared, to re-emerge, as from chrysalids, transformed into this sparkling, desirable form, all things made new.

But as the post-war influx of 'new buses' began to swell, I became aware that terrible things were happening in the land. Many of my old, favourite double-deckers, and the single-deckers with the most interesting runes, were disappearing, were simply vanishing in the night. I guessed they were going to showmen, like the UU registration I had failed to record. I was told there was a scrapyard at Coltishall where many of them rested (and, eventually, I cycled out to investigate). Several re-appeared in various guises, dotted about the countryside, enjoying extended periods of usefulness in extreme old age as caravans, storesheds, workmen's huts, or lorries. Once a location had become known, miles would be cycled to visit it.

These expeditions were akin to pilgrimages. Accompanied usually by a long-suffering friend (one of my former 'drivers'), we stared in wonder and veneration when we reached each shrine. Some which I recall include:

DX 8426 (AH 151) - Rogers' Farm, Norwich Road, Costessey.

NG 3870 (AH 209) - old, dilapidated body in a field at Spixworth. (The chassis was rebodied in 1950).

VG 3110 (L 410) - club-house for bowls club, St Clement's Hill, Norwich.

DX 7512 (P 805) - residence, Bawburgh Lane, Costessey.

DX 7656 (P 812) - builders' site hut, Maple Drive, Waterworks Road, Norwich.

VG 2555 (N 744) - builders' hut, Dereham Road, Costessey, opposite the bottom of Richmond Road.

NG 3874/6/7/80 (AT 930/2/3/6) - lorries, J Billig & Sons, Biltin Works, Salhouse Road, Norwich. NG 3874 was at the Coltishall scrapyard, 14/9/54. I saw NG 3876, NG 3877, and NG 3880 at Salhouse Road, 2/8/54.

APW 856 (P 906) - I nearly repeated my old mistake with UU 5148, for I didn't recognise the registration number; however, it was a Norfolk number, so I noted it. This Tilling-Stevens single-decker had been acquired from Robertson of Stalham in 1936. Allotment shed, just outside Great Yarmouth, on the Acle New Road. It stood a few yards from:

DX 8870 (43) Ipswich Corporation single-decker trolleybus. What a duo!

VF 2795 (J 383) Storeshed, Lower Tharston: I didn't visit this; but I was given a photograph.

VG 5539 (HLG 2) caravan / storeshed at Silfield, Wymondham. The front off-side panel, with registration plate, now adorns my study.

36. Driver Bert Vurley on the Devon and Cornwall Tour with KNG 706 (LS 706), one of the five 'Queen Mary' Bristol LWL6B coaches introduced in 1951.

37. FNG 145 had entered service as LK 8 in November 1945 with an angular Strachan austerity body and traditional clicker boards. As LK 38 it received a new eight-feet-wide highbridge body and was reclassified LKH 38. It is seen at Main Works, Norwich, on its arrival from Eastern Coach Works in May 1953, but took up service as a Cambridge car. (Roger Harrison)

I visited and offered youthful obeisance: but the fascinating stories behind these runes were not yet revealed to me.

In the summer of 1951 - poised between junior school and grammar school - I saw the future. I saw the King's elder daughter, the Princess Elizabeth, when she visited Norwich to declare open the local commemoration of the Festival of Britain.

CNG 204 (LL 504)

was painted for the occasion and fitted with a special headboard. Later, with a different headboard and some deft alterations to the paintwork, it fulfilled the same role at Cambridge.

Then, one morning, more astonishment! A strange-looking double-decker roared unexpectedly up the hill on Service 92. Again, the boundaries of understanding were stretched as I reached for my notebook and waited for the monster to return - because nothing about this bus seemed right, apart from its colour. Had it been anything other than Tilling Red, the whole experience would have been too much. The runes and the side number both broke all the normal rules:

JWT 712 (822).

Where it should have said 'Eastern Counties' it said 'West Yorkshire'; and the radiator looked all wrong; and it sounded different; and the proportions didn't seem right It was, of course, the second Lodekka prototype, which was going round the country 'On Hire' as a demonstrator. It was with Eastern Counties from 28th May until 10th June. I have a photograph of it on Service 89; my best photo shows it on hire to Mansfield District (where it had been in March). I little dreamt what changes this portent heralded.

Then arrived

MAH 744 (LL 744).

In a state of utter awe, I drew it in Thorpe Station yard, on Service 90. It was the second Bristol LS prototype. Had I but known that, seventeen years later, I would drive this vehicle between Soham and Cambridge via the Swaffhams, Bottisham, and Quy on Service 122; that it would be one of our Soham outstation cars; that in the blackness of winter mornings I would grope under each of the nearside panels for the length of coarse string which served as a cold-start; that I myself would be photographed - not drawn! - with this vehicle in 1968 - had I but an inkling of any of these things, the intervening years would all have been wasted as I waited in unbelieving anticipation. It is good not to know too much until we are capable of assimilating and dealing with that knowledge.

In writing so openly, already I have revealed, perhaps, too much. I have disclosed too casually one of the most precious of the sacred numbers, and hinted at its hidden power, and the secret meanings which were revealed only over many years: 744.

VG 2555 (N 744)

> was originally United N 47, acquired from Eastern Motorways in October 1930. It was rebodied by Eastern Counties in 1935 and renumbered N4. In 1946 it was renumbered N 744, and was withdrawn in January 1950. I saw it on a building site in Costessey (as mentioned). The fleet number passed to:

VF 8521 (AH 744)

> - this was a temporary, short-term, out-of-sequence arrangement to make space for the arrival, in October 1950, of

LNG 286 (LK 286).

> AH 744 was a favourite vehicle, whose registration number I had known from earliest times, and which still rolls easily off my tongue. Originally United A 86, it was rebodied by Eastern Coach Works earlier in the year I was born, and became AH 86. In 1946 it was renumbered AH 286. After briefly becoming AH 744, it was withdrawn in 1951 in time for the arrival in July of:

MAH 744 (LL 744)

> - full-fronted and sensational. Unlike any other LL I had ever seen. Withdrawn in 1972, it survives as a preserved vehicle (and an objective, physical expression of my own life and personal history).

This wealth of heritage can be enjoyed by any who stand before it with humility and

38. The long tradition of decorated trams passed only fitfully to the replacing buses, principally because trams could be brilliantly lit from the traction supply but buses could not. A particular effort by Eastern Counties in 1951 was the decoration of CNG 204 (LL 504) for the Festival of Britain celebrations. The scene was in Thorpe Station yard, which for many years was a busy bus terminal in Norwich, and the bus was a 1938 Bristol L4G. After its similar turn of duty at Cambridge, it was withdrawn. (Roger Harrison)

39. The strange proportions of the second Lodekka prototype, West Yorkshire's JWT 712 (822), made it an obvious choice for a photograph when it was spotted on Service 89 at Unthank Road (Neville Street) in May 1951. (Roger Harrison)

understanding, and reflect. Seven four four. 744.

The mantle passed to:

GCL 346N (RLE 744)

- a 1974 Bristol dual-purpose semi-coach - a later equivalent of LE 700. I liked driving these vehicles. Finally,

C744 BEX (MB 744)

- 1986 Mercedes Benz, 20-seater body by Reeve Burgess. Alas, by now the power of the spell was weakening.

6. Dark shadows

My thirteenth year was punctuated by six events of a nature different from anything with which I had had hitherto consciously to come to terms, or to recognise as equal expressions of human experience, as real as the ecstasy and the delight.

1. On 4th December 1951 occurred the Chatham bus disaster. Twenty-three people, mainly youngsters, were killed when, after dark, a bus ploughed into a marching company of Marine cadets. I was appalled. Such depth of emotion, accompanied by an almost personal sense of tragedy was, I believe, a new experience for me, and marked a significant milestone in the process of growing-up.

2. On 6th February 1952 the King died at Sandringham, in Norfolk (Service 35: King's Lynn - Hunstanton, the service on which the most serious Eastern Counties accident had occurred nearby, seven years earlier). I was in the First Form at the City of Norwich School. As I cycled home the news-vendor's flysheet proclaimed: THE KING IS DEAD. I was sad. In those days we all wanted God to save the King. As a fixed point in my wartime-shaped universe, the King was on a par with my TD4s. God had ceased to save the King. But now we wanted Him to save the Queen. Elizabeth the Second! What would the new coins be like?

The King's funeral arrangements were of particular concern to me. In the event, the royal funeral train from Wolferton (the station for Sandringham) to King's Lynn was hauled by an engine of my favourite 'Sandringham' class (remember - A4s didn't come to Norwich!):

61617 *Ford Castle.*

From King's Lynn to King's Cross the train was hauled by the first of the sensations of the previous year:

70000 *Britannia.*

(I expect these details were culled from a surreptitious consultation of 'The Railway Magazine' on W H Smith's book-stall at Thorpe Station.)

3. A few weeks later, on 10th March 1952 - cycling home at the same time of day, and at the same place - I encountered drama even more terrible. I weaved my bike between the traffic trailing back along Castle Meadow; I heard the bells of fire engines, and glimpsed them in the distance at Bank Plain. A single-decker bus had been involved in a fatal accident in Upper King Street and was parked with its near-side front wheel on the pavement, at the bottom of Bank Street. The bus was

KNG 720 (LL 720),

first registered on October 1st 1950, which was operating the 4.15pm Service 5A to Sea Palling via Wroxham and Neatishead; the victim a boy cyclist from Norwich Grammar School.

As I stood by the paper-man, staring along the street, an Aunt appeared. "There's been a dreadful accident," she said. "You don't want to go along there, Jackie."

Grown-ups never get it right. (Someone should submit a thesis on that proven fact.) For, on the contrary, there was nothing I wanted more. I bore her no resentment: she couldn't help being a grown-up; in fact, she was quite a decent sort - the source of the cycle I was leaning against at that very moment. But when she - and the ambulance, which went quietly and without fuss - had both withdrawn, I indulged a small boy's insatiable, even morbid, curiosity, and examined the scene closely. Over the years that followed, I passed along Upper King Street times without number - usually at the wheel of a bus. Only seldom did I fail to recall the horror of that bright afternoon. *Requiescat in pace.*

40. *An air of foreboding hangs over this photograph, in which the fateful Bristol LL5G KNG 720 (LL720) is seen leaving Surrey Street bus station for Sea Palling. When new, this 39-seater was among the Company's first batch of buses built to the newly permitted length of 30 feet. (W J Haynes)*

41. *Some buses are notoriously camera-shy, and VG 5538 (LG 1) was a good example. Here it is caught as it sweeps past the Royal Hotel (off the picture) and into Upper King Street on Service 89. The oncoming vehicle is a 1936 LG on the same route. LG 1 is shown at almost the exact spot where LL 720 was involved in the fatal accident in 1952. (Eastern Daily Press)*

4. On 5th July 1952 the last London tram - car 1951 - ran from Woolwich to New Cross, watched by crowds. This news came as a very great surprise and disappointment: a shock which should have sounded a wake-up call.

London! Even the capital had dispensed with its trams. Those had been the nearest trams to me - and I had failed to see them. But I was 12, not in touch with 'experts', and penniless. There was nothing I could have done, even if I had been forewarned. I'd never been to London. Longing and futility; hope and disappointment; plans and frustrations, all mixed up; ambitions and good intentions vanishing over the horizon - these painful lessons are an integral part of growing up. And I had wanted, so much, to see a Feltham....

5. An experience which affected me deeply occurred on 1st September 1952 when, at the Main Works, I watched - in a kind of disbelief - as some of my TD4s were towed away to the scrapyard at Coltishall, 'life's work well done' (as they say in the obituaries). That afternoon, I plumbed a depth of misery I had never before known. I wanted, badly, to do something about it - to rush forward and explain it was all a terrible mistake, and to put a stop to this wickedness. Instead, I stood mute and miserable. Not only the King: God had failed to save the TD4s, too.

I knew the old Leyland double-deckers were being replaced by the new Bristols - heaven knows, it had been happening for ages. But I think it had never occurred to me, deep down, that one day they would come for my TD4s. I expect I blotted out the knowledge. If you don't think about something it may not happen. But now it was happening, before my very eyes. Side-by-side stood AAH 137, which had posed for the photographer only a few yards away, seventeen years earlier (and four before I was born), and AAH 144. I'm not sure I knew, even then, that they had the blood of the Norwich trams on their hands - if I did, I had long-since forgiven them. They had spoken to me in the womb; they had heralded the dawn of life itself, and heralded each day; they had watched as I slept at night. They had always been there. With nothing else in all creation, apart from my mother, did I feel so intimately connected. This was a bereavement.

6. The Harrow and Wealdstone railway disaster occurred at 8.18 on the morning of 8th October 1952. A local train from Tring to Euston was standing in the station when the overnight express from Perth to Euston, hauled by

46242 *City of Glasgow*

ran into it from behind.

Almost simultaneously, the obstruction was struck by the double-headed 8.00am Euston - Liverpool express, travelling on the down fast lane and hauled by

45637 *Windward Islands* (the pilot engine) and

46202 *Princess Anne.*

The two engines of the Liverpool train mounted the wreckage and overturned. The engine of the Perth train was completely buried in the wreckage, its driver and fireman among the 112 people killed. One week before my thirteenth birthday, this accident left an indelible impression on my mind of the hazards and dangers lurking amid routine duties and innocent delights. I studied the newspaper reports, dismayed that such terrible events could happen. It was partly exciting - but mostly it was terrifying. These reflections, too, were part of my growing up.

Occasionally, something much more cheerful or hopeful happened. For years, the As and AHs had been gradually ousted by LKs and LKHs. At one point, I thought they had all gone; and, indeed, the last might well have been delicensed. I think it likely that an unexpected and temporary car-shortage led to a few being relicensed for a short while. I was tremendously excited to see one again in the Bus Station, on service, when I thought it was dead. This was strong evidence of resurrection. Two of the last survivors with which I was familiar were

FL 8905

which had become AH 755 and lasted until 1953, when it was converted into tree-cutter X 33, and

VE 1994

which was renumbered first A 743, then latterly A 754, and survived until 1954.

42. As mentioned earlier, a blurred and imperfect snapshot can, nonetheless, sometimes capture the essence of an important or memorable moment, or simply of prevailing practices or common sights of long ago which mostly failed to be recorded. Here, for example, is a glimpse of two somewhat different members of the A/AH class. You see the open doorway of the garage in the Surrey Street bus station, with TD4 AAH 137 (AH 233) swinging in towards the pumps, passing rebodied TD1 DX 9021 (A 169) which is on the stand for a relief working.

43. By contrast, this was a scene of almost unbearable sadness, with AAH 137 (AH 233) and AAH 144 (AH 240) waiting at Main Works on 1st September 1952, ready to be towed away to Ben Jordan's scrapyard at Coltishall. The PRIVATE and RELIEF 'destinations' were on a permanent hinged flap forming the back of the indicator aperture into which the clicker-boards were snapped. Service numbers were chalked in the black eyes of the RELIEF boards. (Roger Harrison)

7. Easter in Steelhouse Lane

Another Epiphany lay just around the corner. In Coronation Year, I burst out of East Anglia with a vengeance at Easter. A school-friend and I planned a long cycle ride, staying at youth hostels. His parents wisely saw several drawbacks in our plan. Instead of issuing a veto, they generously adopted a lateral approach, and suggested an alternative: I could accompany them on one of their holiday visits to my friend's grandmother in Birmingham. The Liverpool fantasy was fulfilled. It was a different destination, but the sub-plot was identical. I would see trams.

We travelled by car, and the journey became more exciting the longer it lasted. I tried to absorb every scene and sensation, and savour it all, drink of it deeply, in case it should never happen again. A break at Cambridge gave time only for brief, admiring glances at the colleges. (Eastern Counties buses were here, too, with numbers recognisably part of familiar sequences, but individuals that I, mostly, hadn't seen before, so each bus brought a fresh excitement and sense of discovery.)

Then on to Caxton Gibbet. (I didn't know, then, that one of my beloved LJ coaches had been involved in a serious accident here on the Service N to Birmingham in 1938:

AVF 369 (LJ 19).

The *Daily Mirror* described 'a scene like a battlefield', and several passengers were injured.) On again, intoxicated with wonder: St Neots (just clipping Huntingdonshire); over the A1, where United coaches thundered south towards London, and north to Newcastle; Bedford (John Bunyan!); Northampton (I never forgot the VV registration letters on the red Corporation buses); Coventry (where the car manufacturers' territory began); Elmdon Airport, and into Birmingham along Coventry Road (but too late, alas, for the trolleybuses, which had been withdrawn in 1951). We stayed at Denbigh Road, Bordesley Green, just off the Service 8 (the Inner Circle). Mulliner's coachworks were at the end of the street.

Our trips into town were on the twin Stechford services to Carrs Lane: 53, via Garrison Lane and Fazeley Street, which had replaced the trams on route 90 in 1948, and (my preference) Service 54, via Deritend and Digbeth, which passed the entrance to Coventry Road bus garage and the Midland Red coach station, and had replaced the trams on route 84 at the same time.

On Easter Saturday, 4th April 1953, I walked excitedly up the right hand side of the road leading from Corporation Street towards Snow Hill, knowing the hour was at hand. At the corner, I stopped and looked to the right into Steelhouse Lane. There it was: My first tram!

How to put so much longing, conjecture, and expectation into words is beyond me. Rides were compulsory that week, and my youthful senses were alert to every aspect of this sensual experience. The gliding motion of the car was so unlike a bus. The sounds, too, were utterly different. The ambience was not of these times, but like being transported in, and to, an earlier age. And, to me, frankly - the ambience was not of this world. I sailed upon the wings of the wind.

We came to a roundabout - and sliced through the middle of it. I was astonished and delighted at the simplicity and audacity of it - not round the roundabout: clean through the middle. We passed the studios of the BBC Midland Region (where, I was told, 'The Archers' was recorded); Aston Street became Aston Road before we came to a halt at Aston Cross, beside Ansell's Brewery.

Then, onward - but, oh! There were too many impressions to take in and to capture. For I was living in the last days. This time there would definitely be no second chance, once the holiday was over. Most of the tramway system had been abandoned. These were the last routes, and they hadn't long to go.

My sadness and outrage were equalled only by my impotence. But now was not then - not quite; now was for living, for getting, for exploring, and for remembering, affectionately, tenderly, gratefully, and for ever. At Gravelly Hill, the three last routes divided. We visited each terminus: to the left, the 78 went off up Slade Road to Short Heath; ahead, the 2 continued along Gravelly Hill to Erdington; while, to the right, the 79 sped on a long section of reserved track to Pype Hayes Park. What wonderful parks this city had!

My friend described all the reserved track there used to be on Bristol Road South, out to Longbridge, Rednal, and Rubery which I had just missed,.... This 'just missing' was a phenomenon I

44. I had no camera to capture the wonder of seeing my first tram: no way of obtaining a photograph to treasure forever - so I am indebted to the unknown photographer who took this view of 1925 Birmingham car 693 in just the spot where that encounter took place. The kerbside loading bay, the information board, and buses like the 1938 front-entrance Midland Red double-decker EHA287 (2155) were interesting too.

45. Another part of the city with a carefully thought - out tramway layout was Aston Cross, complete with superb decorative clock. Car 577, photographed on 7th June 1952, was an older vehicle dating from 1914. This and 693 were both on the Erdington Service 2, and still in service at the time of my visit. (John H Meredith)

was beginning to recognise as a cosmic element I resented deeply.

But, for now, there was a breathlessness about it all. I had made contact, at last. (Almost too late - but *just* in time). It was a consummation - though, at the time, I didn't know the meaning of the word. A tryst had been kept; a promise honoured. The stories of open-top, 3ft 6in gauge, purple (or was it chocolate?) tramcars which once roamed the streets of Norwich (till they were banished by the TD4s); the stories of Felthams, Green Goddesses, and, best of all, those magically coloured Coronations and Cunarders with which FYS 494 was even now, surely, a working partner on equal terms; these, and countless photographs, articles, reminiscences and recollections had more than whetted my appetite: they had created a vision, an ideal, a kind of holy quest - and at last, *at last*, I had found that in which my soul delighted. But I knew I would not pass that way again.

Thus was the experience heightened, intensified, and tinged with a kind of desperate sadness. The Lord had given; but the Lord would soon be taking away. I soaked in all I could that week, greedily, hungrily. It was joy and fulfilment and everything that I had wondered about and hoped for. I marvelled and rejoiced. I couldn't believe it would all soon be in the past, and these living creatures mercilessly destroyed and consigned to history. I knew that all things come to an end; AAH 137 was at Coltishall. But did it have to end so soon? It was too cruel. We had only just met. This was an Epiphany indeed, with myrrh hidden among the gold and frankincense.

We haunted one other venue (apart from Snow Hill station with its GWR engines), the first visit being on that Easter Saturday evening: Digbeth Coach Station. I knew Midland Red was a great company, and its coaches were a familiar sight in Norwich during the summer months, especially on the Leicester - Great Yarmouth service, which we called L but they (for some reason) called V.

During this holiday week, I established a first-hand, personal rapport with this famous company, which possessed such a distinguished place in the bus world, designing its own distinctive buses and operating over a vast area I could scarcely imagine, from Hereford, Worcester, and Banbury, to Shrewsbury, Stafford, and Leicester. I admired its history, which began with horse buses in Birmingham at the turn of the 20th Century, and its great sense of tradition. I loved the fact that 'Midland Red' was almost an affectionate nickname and that, when necessary, the company could produce a dignified title of impressive solemnity: 'The Birmingham and Midland Motor Omnibus Company Limited'.

But that Saturday evening at Digbeth coach station and garage will - like the Steelhouse Lane experience earlier - live with me for ever. There were coaches arriving, or parked-up, from every corner of the kingdom. The different liveries, the names (Yorkshire Woollen - that was a new one!), the entire atmosphere was in a league different from anything I had known previously. I learnt that evening (though I didn't put it into words) how utterly provincial and restricted my knowledge and experience had been, and how limited. The 'feel' of Digbeth was something new and special. The Midland Red buses included a single-decker which looked very old.

Our access was unimpeded; we squeezed with impunity and breathless wonderment between vehicles creaking and cooling after their long journeys, and passengers being greeted (in a very strange accent!) by waiting relatives. And there, amid it all, was an LJ coach of Eastern Counties, which had stood in Surrey Street that very morning, and had been making the journey to Birmingham on Service N, even as I was experiencing my first tram-ride. Those beautiful but ageing coaches would not make many more journeys on Service N.

I experienced a pang as I stood before it, as if, in some way, I was being unfaithful by being so rapturously happy on alien territory, and it had caught me, and reproached in a silent rebuke. Or I might just have been slightly homesick.

Coronation Year stands out in my memory for several other reasons. In May, another new bus appeared 'on hire'. It was very smart indeed, and in the Tilling green livery of United Counties. It was the first Bristol Lodekka I had seen in its more finished state (its front quite unlike West Yorkshire 822 - though I'm not sure I connected the two vehicles). I copied the numbers carefully:

JBD 955 (950).

That year brought the last batch of (eight) highbridge double-deckers. I remember distinctly at Thorpe Station, on the way to school, noting with approval an impressive new rune:

46. Out in the suburbs, the tramway reserved tracks were particularly impressive. This section on Streetly Road was the approach to the Short Heath terminus, with 1921 car 636 on 7th June 1953. It would all be abandoned less than a month later. (John H Meredith)

47. Back home in Norwich among all the red buses, an apparition in green turned up the following month, May 1953. This was the United Counties Lodekka JBD 955 (950), seen here arriving in Surrey Street Bus Station on Service 12 from Attleborough and Wymondham. Its appearance was truly revolutionary! (Roger Harrison)

OVF 171 (LKH 171).

So they were still being purchased! (and would last long enough for me to drive: but that - perhaps fortunately - I didn't know). However, I knew United Counties 950 symbolised the future.

Another stunning glimpse of things to come was the arrival of

OAH 750 (LS 750)
OAH 751 (LS 751)
OAH 752 (LS 752)
OAH 753 (LS 753)
OAH 754 (LS 754)
OAH 755 (LS 755).

I understood instinctively that these wonderful new coaches, with their under-floor engines, sounded the death-knell for the half-cab LJs I had known from the dawn of time when, amid the chaos, they were grey. Although I was not yet 14, the realisation had dawned that exciting new advances are frequently marred by a corresponding loss. I doubt if I perceived that the arrival of my LJs, some eighteen years earlier, had had exactly the same effect on vehicles I would have given my right hand to have seen. I found it very interesting, though, to see that LS 750 and LS 753 were in 'Metropolitan' livery. I was surprised but not bewildered; even then, the concepts of goodwill, continuity and familiarity made sense.

I was fortunate enough to be included in another visit to Birmingham in the autumn. We took the bus to Aston Cross, and wandered disconsolately past the brewery, up Park Road, along Witton Lane, and beside the Aston Villa football ground to Witton Depot. Part of it was open, and the public allowed to purchase any such various items as appealed. The atmosphere was hushed and funereal. I bought a wing mirror, which I have to this day, and picked up a torn notice (which I framed, only recently, to ensure continued safe preservation):

BIRMINGHAM CITY TRANSPORT
ALTERATION OF
TRANSPORT SERVICES
ERDINGTON, SHORT HEATH
AND PYPE HAYES

During the morning of Saturday, 4th July, 1953, Motor Omnibuses will replace the Tramcars on the Erdington, Short Heath and Pype Hayes Services

The last Tramcars will leave Steelhouse Lane at 10.30am.

We came away, clutching miserably our humble mementoes. Ichabod - the glory of the Lord had departed! One afternoon, that week, we went by car to Stratford-upon-Avon. As we arrived, we passed a scrapyard. There, to our horror, stood a row of broken, blue ghosts. The glory had departed to Stratford-upon-Avon - but it was glorious no more.

8. The Rosary and The Dell

Yards from my birthplace - and with a 92 bus-stop at its entrance - was the Rosary Cemetery. It was the first non-denominational cemetery in England when it was opened in 1821. Sloping, well-wooded, and covered with crocuses in the spring, it remains one of my favourite places. The mood is timeless, and I spent hours playing there as a child, searching for chestnuts and conkers, and studying the inscriptions on tombstones. (Two commemorated John Prior and James Light, driver and fireman respectively of the Yarmouth Mail train, who were killed in the famous Thorpe Railway disaster of 10th September 1874. By a misunderstanding at Norwich (Thorpe) Station, the express from London was allowed to proceed on the single track, and the two trains collided head-on.)

48. The 'OVF' batch of LKHs was the last of a series which for Eastern Counties had commenced in 1944, based on the several varieties of the Bristol K-type chassis. This final style, eight feet wide and with Eastern Coach Works body, was a classic design much beloved of enthusiasts almost everywhere, and OVF 171 (LKH 171) was worthy of an official photograph at Main Works when new in October 1953. It was a KSW5G and ran until 1971. As for Service 17, it dated back to United's acquisition of local Great Eastern Railway bus services in 1920, which in turn had originated in 1905 as we shall see later.

49. Greater excitement had however been engendered by the first of the new underfloor-engined Bristol LS6B coaches in July 1953. This was OAH 752 (LS 752), taken on tour by driver Bert Vurley and seen here at Torquay.

At the Rosary, the only difficulty was gaining admission. Old Palmer, the keeper, was best avoided. There were parallels with Ben Jordan's scrapyard a few miles away at The Dell, Coltishall, to which I cycled, with a friend, from time to time. In all fairness, admission was usually granted: then the wonder began. At The Dell, hundreds of old cars, buses, and lorries lay decomposing in natural surroundings. It possessed almost a sacred nature, like an ancestral burial ground; to enter was to encounter a choice and heady blend of excitement and sadness.

Here it was possible magically to re-enter the past, renew old acquaintances, and experience mystical communion. Here - unbelievably - were the recognisable forms of familiar, long-lost, much loved friends: friends who were the most tangible, meaningful symbols of life as I had known and experienced it. Yet they were decaying before my eyes, overgrown with bindweed, ivy, and nettles like the graves in the Rosary Cemetery. I was helpless to respond to their wistful appeals and last-gasp supplications; and their strength was almost gone.

50. These are the graves in the Rosary Cemetery, Thorpe Hamlet, Norwich, of one of the engine crews killed in the Thorpe railway disaster of 1874. The campion and cow parsley provide a tranquil springtime setting. At the Rosary, far into the future, I would bury Alan England, a popular young driver and enthusiast.

At Coltishall, in early adolescence, I sensed important truths and learned some bitter lessons: that all things pass away, nothing stays the same forever, and there can never be any going back - except in that dimension ruled by the heart and the mind. At Coltishall, I clutched at childhood, and felt it slipping away through despairing, grasping fingers. Contemplating my TD4s was like being in the family crypt. On one exciting occasion, for a few pence I came away with a front registration number plate: NG 1918, and a rear plate: AVF 353. Each had been hanging, as by a thread; today, they survive as holy relics. Recently, at Norwich library, I viewed a short piece of film taken from the front of a car being driven round the streets of Norwich in 1950 - and had the curious experience of following my very own AVF 353 rear number plate the length of Magdalen Street!

On Tuesday 14th September 1954 I was permitted to explore The Dell and noted the following former Eastern Counties buses. All are Leyland TD1 double-deckers unless stated otherwise:

GH 3818 (KS 904) 1930 AEC Regal coach. This body 1940. Ex-Clarke's of Felixstowe, 1951. Green livery.

NG 5404 (AH 213) 1933 TD2. Never rebodied.

VG 5545 (HLG 8) 1933 Bristol. Ex-Norwich Electric Tramways.

AVF 353 (HLG 11) 1936 Bristol.

51. At The Dell, Coltishall, a Broads village about seven miles north of Norwich, nature seemed to offer similar solace to these departed Leyland TD1s. They were an interesting pair, with DX 9022 (A 170) having been new to 'the Road Car' in December 1930, and NG 1911 (A 176) of January 1932 numerically the first new vehicle purchased by the Eastern Counties Omnibus Company. Both were rebodied in November 1939 and withdrawn in 1950. (Maurice Doggett)

AAH 140 (AH 236) 1935 TD4.

FNG 145 (LK 38). The 1945 Strachan body. (The chassis was rebodied in 1953.)

VF 8516 (AH 273) 1930 Ex-United. This body 1938.

NG 2731 (AH 196) 1932 TD2. This body 1940.

FL 8902 (A 339) 1930 Ex-Peterborough Traction. This body 1937.

VF 8509 (A 266) 1930 Ex-U. This body 1938.

ER 8807 (AH 263) 1928 Ex-Ortona. This body 1937.

VE 2039 (A 317) 1929 Ex-O. This body 1937.

DX 7654 (X 29) 1928 Tilling-Stevens. Ex-Eastern Counties Road Car Co. Originally a normal-control coach. Rebodied 1935. Previously P 810, and to lorry 1949.

VF 9980 (X 23) 1930 Tilling-Stevens sd. Ex-U. P 18. Withdrawn 1944 and converted to lorry.

NG 2727 (AH 192) 1932 TD2. This body 1940.

MV 983 (KD 131) 1931 AEC Regent. Ex-NET. This body 1940.

ER 8805 (AH 326) 1928 Ex-O. This body 1937, but rebuilt after war damage in 1943, and reclassified as a highbridge vehicle.

DX 8421 (AH 146) 1929 Ex-ECRCC. This body 1938.

DX 8357 (AH 742) 1929 Ex-ECRCC. Rebodied 1937. Damaged by enemy action in 1942. Rebuilt and reclassified as a highbridge vehicle AH 142. Renumbered 1949, to make way for LKH 142.

DX 9023 (A 171) 1930 Ex-ECRCC. This body 1939.

FL 8901 (AH 338) 1930 Ex-P. This body 1938.

VG 3152 (A 218) 1930 Ex-NET. This body 1939.

DX 8423 (A 148) 1930 Ex-ECRCC. This body 1938.

VF 8518 (AH 275) 1930 Ex-U. This body 1939.

NG 1918 (A 183) 1932. Never rebodied.

NG 1920 (A 185) 1932. Never rebodied.

DX 8358 (AH 143) 1929 Ex-ECRCC. This body 1937. Rebuilt after war damage, in 1942, and reclassified as a highbridge vehicle.

NG 1911 (A 176) 1932. This body 1939.

DX 9022 (A 170) 1930 Ex-ECRCC. This body 1939.

DX 9021 (A 169) 1930 Ex-ECRCC. This body 1939.

NG 2733 (A 198) 1932 TD2. Never rebodied.

GNG 520 (LM 490). This 1936 body had been built for ex-United F20. In 1947 it was transferred to a new Bristol chassis. In 1951 the new chassis received a new body: LL 490.

VG 5542 (HLG 5) 1933 Bristol. Ex-NET.

NG 1912 (A 177) 1932. This body 1939.

VE 4200 (AH 314) 1930 Ex-O. This body 1939.

VG 3153 (A 219) 1930 Ex-NET. This body 1939.

DX 9025 (A 173) 1930 Ex-ECRCC. This body 1939.

AAH 141 (AH 237) 1935 TD4.

AAH 138 (AH 234) 1935 TD4.

AAH 143 (AH 239) 1935 TD4.

AAH 139 (AH 235) 1935 TD4.

NG 1914 (A 179) 1932. This body 1940.

VF 8538 (X 22) 1930 Tilling Stevens Ex-U. Previously P 17. Withdrawn 1944 and converted to lorry.

VG 5540 (HLG 3) 1933 Bristol. Ex-NET.

ER 8804 (AH 752) 1928 Ex-O. This body 1937. Until 1951, AH 302. Renumbered to make way for LK 302.

BVF 635 (LD 415) 1937 Bristol sd.

VG 5544 (HLG 7) 1933 Bristol. Ex-NET.

VE 2042 (A 753) 1929 Ex O. This body 1937. A 303 until 1951. Renumbered to make way for LK 303.

DX 9026 (A 174) 1931 Ex-ECRCC. This body, 1939.

VE 1994 (A 754) 1929 Ex-O. This body 1937. A 281, twice renumbered 1950: A 743 for LK 281, 1951: A 754 for LL 743.

AAH 144 (AH 240) 1935 TD4.

VF 8514 (AH 285) 1930 Ex-U. This body 1938.

AVF 356 (HLG 14) 1936 Bristol.

AAH 142 (AH 238) 1935 TD4.

DX 9020 (A 168) 1930 Ex-ECRCC. This body 1939.

AAH 137 (AH 233) 1935 TD4.

NG 3874 (AT 930) 1933 Leyland TS4 sd. Had been withdrawn 1950, sold, and converted to a lorry. This time it would be scrapped.

Fifty-seven hulks - some, bodies only; many, engines missing; a few, more-or-less complete. I've not revised the order: this is how they rested as I wandered and clambered among them, that bright morning. Today, 'Health and Safety' alone would have denied me one of the great experiences of my young life. (I wish I could repeat it.)

9. Summer days

I was approaching 15; my understanding was gathering momentum. From the small legal writing on the sides of vehicles I obtained addresses of other companies, and wrote requesting fleet lists and leaflets. Trent and Midland General - to name two - were very helpful. Lincolnshire gave me the address of the Omnibus Society; Maidstone and District suggested that the PSV Circle might also be able to help. I was gaining access to sources of authoritative information.

Most importantly, I came to understand more clearly how Eastern Counties had been formed from a merger of the East Anglian (mostly Norfolk) section of United Automobile Services Ltd;

52. GH 3818 (KS 904) was a 1930 rebodied AEC Regal Green Line coach which eventually became No. 3 with Clarke's of Felixstowe, and passed to Eastern Counties in December 1951. It never received EC livery and went to Coltishall in 1952. (Collection of the late Tony Norris)

53. A last look at two rebodied ex-Ortona TD1s, VE 1994 and VE 2042 (A 754/3), flanked by AAH 144 (AH 240) and VG 5544 (HLG 7). (Maurice Doggett)

54. The first four Eastern Counties Lodekkas arrived in 1954. SAH 232 (LKD 232) was in the second batch, new in March 1955. This official photograph illustrates clearly the original full-depth radiator grille and mudguards, later amended. The fact that engineers arranged the photograph is betrayed by the fact that the destination screen is set incorrectly! Service 34 travelled via Dereham and Swaffham; Shipdham was served by the 13.

Eastern Counties Road Car Company Ltd of Ipswich; Ortona Motor Company Ltd of Cambridge; and the Peterborough Electric Traction Company Ltd. Astoundingly, it turned out that our United *was* the same as the Grange Road, Darlington company. However, it was not until the PSV Circle Fleet History appeared in 1958 that the full picture, including the subsequent acquisitions, became clear. Then long-sought knowledge brought deep satisfaction, a sense of exhilaration, and something akin to a peace that passeth all understanding. However, trams remained as far away as ever. Birmingham had whetted my appetite; like Oliver, I longed for more.

The process which had begun when West Yorkshire 822 roared past my house, up the hill, on Service 92 in 1951 reached its climax on Saturday 17th July 1954 when I recorded the first Eastern Counties Lodekka:

OVF 227 (LKD 227).

It was on the 8.45am Service 34 from King's Lynn, which operated on summer Saturdays beyond Norwich and on to Great Yarmouth via the Acle New Road (the direct road across the marshes, not the route of the Service 7 Norwich - Great Yarmouth, which followed the old road through the villages).

In the days before by-passes became universal, I spent idyllic Saturday afternoons during the summer at a spot on Thorpe Road, not far from my house, where the A47 from Yarmouth split into two: Thorpe Road, to the right, continued into the city (and to the Bus Station proper); Carrow Road, to the left, passed the Norwich City football ground and formed part of the ring road. It also gave access to the road at the top of the Bus Station, where some of the Service X7 Trent coaches picked up (but didn't enter the Bus Station itself). The streams of old Trent, Midland General, and Mansfield District coaches (in red, blue, and green livery respectively) were a cause of enormous satisfaction and pleasure. I have the numbers still. That was where I learned that RC was a Derby registration, and wrestled with destinations like Heanor, Hucknall, Pinxton, and Sutton - in - Ashfield.

This almost continuous stream of coaches - heading towards Yarmouth in the morning, and back in the afternoon - constituted, to a schoolboy, free entertainment of the highest order. On Saturday 14th August 1954, I noted 39 Trent, 8 Midland General, 5 Mansfield and District, and 2 Barton Transport.

Also in the procession that afternoon were 3 Lincolnshire, 11 United Counties, 4 Sheffield United

55. KPW 373 (CS 989) was a 1949 Commer Avenger, acquired from W Rasberry of Grimston near King's Lynn in January 1951. When this photograph was taken in Surrey Street garage, in 1957, it was standing beside GNG 272 (X 24), a Ford V8 recovery lorry, but the coach was allocated to Peterborough depot, and had brought passengers to Norwich for the Royal Show. (Ivan Ames)

Tours, and 14 York Bros, with 12 Midland Red heading for Leicester and a further 2 for Birmingham (I could picture their destination). The Midland Red coaches seemed, somehow, superior - far newer, and sleeker in every way. They were allowed *in* the Bus Station.

To that long list of coaches must be added the vehicles of smaller, private operators which were almost too numerous to record. They included, that day, 16 on hire to the larger companies. For example, Farrow of Melton Mowbray had two coaches on hire to Trent, and Straw of Leicester had two on hire to Midland Red.

Eastern Counties had coaches on hire from Longland of Crowland, Delaine of Bourne, Patch of Stamford, and Norfolk Coachways of Attleborough. United had four from Simpson of Ripon, which were being shepherded by

EHN 988 (LLT 13).

But the vehicles for which I waited most eagerly were those Eastern Counties coaches from recently acquired operators which were allocated to the Company's western area and therefore not so familiar to eastern area observers - vehicles like the Peterborough based:

KPW 373 (CS 989) Commer Avenger
JPW 259 (AS 960) Leyland
JBJ 833 (FS 998) Foden.

FS 998 had become my favourite Eastern Counties vehicle, for the reasons which, by now, will be familiar: the shape, the sound, the make, the history, the registration number, the magical fleet number. FS 998 and AS 960 were on Service L that afternoon.

August Bank Holiday (then the first Monday of the month) was, for the enthusiast, a major festival. In my larger red Woolworth's notebook there are original entries, scribbled in pencil, of observations made from 6.30pm to 9.45pm at Thorpe Road on Monday 1st August 1955. Traffic was very heavy, with thirty Eastern Counties single-deckers returning from the coast on excursions. In addition, a constant stream of (mostly) double-deckers (I counted over twenty) ran light to Great

I was excited to see United

DHN 442 (LLT 2)

caught up in this non-stop operation, with an 'On Hire to Eastern Counties' sticker in the window. I found it gratifying to know that United was operating again on Service 7! At such hectic times - with crowds to be returned to the city - any vehicle standing in the garage at Great Yarmouth or at Norwich was pressed into service if a crew could be found. Coincidentally, on the previous day I had noted Eastern Counties

EX 6657 (DS 982)

heading for Great Yarmouth bearing an 'On Hire to United Auto Sers' sticker, which suggested that it had been employed in similar fashion while in the north of England on Service S.

On these busy days, I found there were occasional lulls in the intensity of the traffic, and brief quiet times when coaches would speed past only singly. Then an explosion of action would occur as the next wave of coaches appeared, often nose-to-tail, and testing severely the recording skills of the observer.

The operator whose coaches presented the most formidable challenge was York Bros, of Northampton, whose vehicles were named after ships of the Royal Navy. There were thus three details to record: registration number, fleet number, and name. With vehicles in convoy the task was impossible, and my York Bros fleet list was compiled only over a period of time, was never completed, and may contain inaccuracies. But the names, and their significance, possessed a two-fold educational value. What was the history of the ship and where had it seen action? And why had those names been chosen in the first instance: was it because Glasgow, Liverpool, and Sheffield had trams?! What was a centaur? Who were Perseus and Theseus?

YORK BROS, NORTHAMPTON

19	PRR 72	HMS Berwick
24	FBD 200	HMS Cumberland
26	GNV 900	HMS King George V
27	GRP 800	HMS Theseus (1954)
28	HBD 400	HMS Compass Rose
29	JRP 2	HMS Bulwark
30	JRP 3	HMS Centaur
33	CRP 801	HMS Sheffield
34	DRP 1	HMS Duke of York
35	EBD 1	HMS Glasgow
36	EBD 2	HMS Gloucester
37	EBD 3	HMS Southampton
38	EBD 4	HMS Birmingham
39	ENV 500	HMS Liverpool
41	FNV 700	HMS Superb
42	FNV 701	HMS Ceylon
43	FRP 100	HMS Kenya
44	FRP 101	HMS Dido
45	GNV 700	HMS Ark Royal
46	GNV 701	HMS Eagle
48	HBD 102	HMS Victorious
49	JBD 100	HMS Hermes
50	FNV 1	HMS Dorsetshire
51	FNV 702	HMS Ocean
52	FNV 703	HMS Unicorn
53	JBD 101	HMS Swiftsure
54	LNV 301	HMS Implacable
55	LNV 302	HMS Perseus

56. United's DHN 442 (LLT 2) was a 1938 Brush-bodied Leyland TS8. By 1954 it had been supplanted from the London services and had had the "Tyne Tees Thames" panels removed from the body sides, whereupon it spent two summers (1954 and 1955) based at Ripon. This was primarily to provide duplication between Leeds and Lowestoft, and here it was waiting time on waste ground off Saville Street in the centre of Leeds, with the crew on board and the screens set to "Doncaster, Lowestoft". On the open road it was an impressive sight to behold. (D F Parker)

57. For passengers to or from Newcastle, the refreshment stop at Doncaster was important. Those on Yarmouth-bound Dennis Lancet EX 6657 (DS 982) seem ready to be on their way after their break, and the 1950 Duple coach body doubtless made for a comfortable ride. The vehicle had come to Eastern Counties from Metropolitan Coaches in 1951.

56	LNV 303	HMS Indefatigable
60	KNV 300	HMS Indomitable
61	LRP 700	HMS Albion
62	LRP 701	HMS Theseus (1955)

So, the wide-eyed infant became the observant child, who became the boyish enthusiast, who turned into the knowledgeable adolescent. All are me; and all were driven by curiosity, and by a compulsion to understand. Now, when I consult the notes I compiled fifty-five years ago, a youth is instructing an old man, like Jesus in the temple. The old man, also, is me.

10. Christ of the Kelvin Hall

Early in 1955 I wrote my first letter to the local press: a eulogistic tribute to the bus company, currently undergoing one of its regular bouts of public criticism. Pennies were tight in our house, and the *Evening News* was not purchased regularly. However, the kindly Glasheens usually pushed their copy through our letter-box, later in the evening. When the paper arrived on this historic occasion, I found, to my indignation, that a large cross had been pencilled across my precious letter - whether to draw attention to it, or as an expression of dissent, I never discovered.

The school trip to Derbyshire in May 1955 provided an exciting opportunity to see Trent buses operating on their own territory. (Incidentally, I had still not yet visited London.)

I noted hundreds of numbers in a week which included a visit to the Manchester Ship Canal, when the different, yet similar, liveries of Manchester Corporation, Stockport Corporation, and North Western again tested the accuracy of my powers of observation to the utmost. These records included two East Midland buses:

HVO 851 (D51) at Derby

BAL 601 (N1) at Monsal Head

in their strange yellow-and-brown livery, which I didn't like. I might have taken a different view, however, had I known that this was the pre-1930 livery of the old United, retained by East Midland (which was a direct historical descendant of the Underwood branch of the United empire).

However, my teenage life was on the point of undergoing a dramatic and decisive change of direction. At the age of 15½ years, and from a non-churchgoing background, I experienced an evangelical Christian conversion. The details surrounding this event are a separate story, but two facts should be noted. Firstly, I never went back on the decision I made on 28th April 1955. Religion became the primary focus of my life and everything else effectively became subordinate to it. This was neither brain-washing nor fanaticism; it was good, positive, exhilarating, and liberating.

I was, by temperament, a natural catholic, and therefore never in any serious danger of becoming narrow-minded or sectarian; but I delighted in my discovery - which was not the discovery of all the answers, but a framework which provided concepts and language to ask the right questions, and explore possibilities.

This new discovery assumed naturally that its rightful place in my life was at its heart and centre, and that its claims took priority. With those assumptions I concurred, eagerly. Buses and trams were not banished. They were incorporated. In their incorporation they lost nothing of their validity and potency as channels of insight and truth.

Secondly, my conversion came from Scotland. The All-Scotland Crusade, 1955, was led by the American evangelist, Billy Graham. Its packed rallies were relayed (not televised!) to various centres across the country, including Norwich. I had recently become attached to a church near my home, and all the young people were encouraged to attend - with the aforementioned result.

The beauty of Jesus and the attractiveness of his Kingdom of Love overwhelmed me. This was the Way I wanted to walk in - wherever it should lead. Had I but known....

The crusade was held in - and the preaching that converted me came from - the Kelvin Hall in Glasgow. Glasgow - filled with all those buses and trams painted like my vision on the Heath. My teenage body, with its competing claims and demands, was in Norwich; my heart was in heaven - and, partly, at the western end of Argyle Street. I had not reached Glasgow but, for the second time,

58. At the time of my 1955 visit to Derbyshire, the Leyland PD2/12 was the current double-deck standard in the Trent fleet. This one, with Leyland body, was CRC 833 (1233) of 1951, and was photographed at Huntingdon Street, Nottingham, ready to depart on the busy trunk route 8. (Photo: G H F Atkins / © courtesy John Banks collection)

59. Two worlds are combined for me in this photograph of Glasgow's Kelvin Hall, showing (on the right) the place from which I first heard the call to Christian conversion, and showing an orange, green and cream tram going past. Visible on the left is the Glasgow Museum and Art Gallery, Kelvingrove, where Salvador Dali's famous 'Christ of St John of the Cross' is displayed. In the foreground the parapets of the bridge over the River Kelvin mark the point where the Cunarder tram will run from Argyle Street into Dumbarton Road on its journey to Scotstoun. (J E Gready / Lens of Sutton)

Glasgow had come to me. My youthful sincerity and vulnerability were no match for *Just As I Am*, sung to the shamelessly heart-tugging *Woodworth*. And I am glad.

Ten years later, old Duncan McIntosh - who sang in the massed choir - gave me his crusade Song Book when he heard my story. A drawing of the Kelvin Hall adorns the tartan cover. Now he's in heaven (and his dear wife), and I hold his book and look at his name, and wonder if the book has been on a tram, on the way to choir rehearsals....

Each day, when school was over, I worked as a grocery delivery boy. In my heart, my trade-bike - with deep carrier, and small wheel at the front - was really a double-decker.

One of my regular deliveries, each Saturday morning, was to Jack Brereton and his wife, Monica. They had always lived fairly near, and I couldn't remember a time when I didn't know them. They were not family friends, but mother would always stop in the street to talk with Mrs Brereton who, in my childish manner, I thought very beautiful and kind. Jack Brereton was the Chief Storekeeper at Main Works and, discovering my interest, generously spent the morning of Sunday 26th February 1956 giving me a personal guided tour. Everywhere was silent, like a great cathedral; only a watchman and two storemen, I think, were on duty.

For me, the entire occasion possessed a surreal quality, like a dream. There I was, in the middle of it all, an invited guest, with no need to be on edge waiting for the challenging shout of a watching chargehand. And when, in the body shop, I was allowed to sit in the cab of

FNG 821 (LKH 59)

I was overwhelmed with indescribable bliss. I felt no guilt for missing church that morning. To sit in the cab! It was a 'first' which I've never forgotten.

But another Epiphany moment was not far away. On Monday 16th April 1956, around mid-day, I approached Harvey Lane on my cycle, along Gordon Avenue. At the junction I stopped, looked right, looked left, and - and I thought I must be ill! Approaching, after climbing the steep hill which forms the southern half of Harvey Lane, was a vision with which I was not equipped to cope. It was unexpected, and I was unprepared. Even at 16, I stared open-mouthed, trying to assimilate the experience and record details at the same time.

It was a freshly-painted Leyland TD1, with outside stairs and in full Eastern Counties livery. I had seen nothing like it - not even, I think, (at that time) in photographs. Had I made no progress at all? Great Yarmouth blue, when I was two; the vision on the heath, when I should have been going home for dinner - they had posed great problems in their day, but I had overcome them. But this time-machine, this wizardry, this image of days long gone defied analysis. Why couldn't it have happened in Fishergate? I was willing it to happen in Fishergate, in the murky depths of the dust-cart depot. I would have been serene, and radiant and complete.

On Harvey Lane, in the spring sunshine, I was thrown utterly. First, my mind went blank; then it felt excitement beyond words (once I had won time enough to become excited). Above all, I was mystified. I was mystified in that delicious, profound, and wondering way which lies at the innermost heart of enthusiasm - and at the heart of *all* our quests for meaning. There is no progress in any worthwhile human endeavour without these strange experiences of surprise, reverence, and mystery.

DR 4902 (A 001).

With the experience of years I managed, even at point-blank range, to capture both numbers. Was this the first of a large new batch of similar vehicles, defying chronology, common sense, progress, and weather? I hoped, but without hope. The fleet number looked suspiciously like an April Fool's jest, a little delayed. The registration number, however, posed no problem. I recognised it immediately. It was Plymouth.

Two former Plymouth Corporation Leyland double-deckers had been obtained by Eastern Counties in 1945; I had known both vehicles well, and liked them:

DR 7402 (A 245)

DR 9837 (AH 244)

- but they did not look like this apparition. Were Plymouth Corporation shedding more vehicles?

It took me a long time to solve this conundrum. The explanation, when it came, was found in the pages of *Buses Illustrated*. DR 4902 was originally Southern National 2849, and first registered on

60. This is FNG 821 (LKH 59) at Peterborough in a photograph which provides a reminder of the vast operating area of the Eastern Counties company, as well as reminding me of the day when as a 16-year-old I sat in the cab. Note the clicker-boards awaiting use or collection, and the intriguing array of parked coaches.

61. The open-staircase Leyland TD1 DR 4902 (A 001) turned many heads and provoked puzzled glances when it appeared on the streets of Norwich in 1956. At the time, it was being restored for preservation. (Eastern Counties)

25th March 1929. It was used later by Chivers and Son of Histon, to ferry workers to and from the fields of their fruit farms in Cambridgeshire, then presented to the British Transport Commission for preservation.

Some thought it a pity the vehicle was not restored to the blue livery of Southern National. They would have denied me my Epiphany!

This story is significant. It represents my last experience of the total, innocent, incomprehension and unalloyed wonder of the enthusiast who looks in from outside, and is eagerly, almost pathetically grateful for any small scrap of information which might shed light on the objects of his veneration. (Incidentally, in that state he is highly vulnerable to *mis*information, from people who *think* they know.) In my case, that relationship was about to change.

11. *Office boy*

The end of schooldays beckoned. I was 16, and wanted to work in the industry which had possessed me since childhood. I wanted to work for Eastern Counties. Jack Brereton recommended me to the company; my application was successful, and my employment began on 13th August 1956. My diary contains many details of bus matters over the following three years; but, mostly, they must be for another day.

It gave me deep satisfaction to have been introduced to the company by Jack Brereton, who had himself joined the Eastern Counties Road Car Company at Ipswich in 1919, the year of its formation. He had documents to prove it (which, later, he entrusted to me). I always felt that, through him, I had a direct link to the earliest days of Eastern Counties - a kind of apostolic succession.

I spent two (rather boring) months in the Traffic Audit department at Head Office but, mercifully, was then transferred to Surrey Street Bus Station as clerk to the Depot Mechanical Superintendent. It was boyhood fantasy come true. I sat in a tiny office beside the DMS. Alec Mortimer had come through the ranks, and led from the front: his white coat was usually covered in grease, and he loved nothing better than to solve a problem himself. It was leadership I greatly admired: the chair beside me was often empty.

I looked out on a row of busy pits used for routine inspections, running repairs, and Public Service Vehicle / Certificate of Fitness inspections (by men from the Ministry). Surrey Street had been the largest single-span garage in the country when it opened in 1936, and the summer vehicle allocation was in the region of 200 vehicles.

Often, some of the fitters allowed me to squeeze into the cab beside them, and steer as we reversed a bus off the pits and back into the ranks. My diary contains excited entries like that for Friday 8th March 1957: "Drove LKH 97! Harry Vardigans did the pedal work - I steered!" Harry and another fitter, Ivan Ames, were keen photographers. One weekend they visited Crowland Abbey (Service 333) and shortly afterwards, I was presented with two photographs: 'The skull of the Abbot Theodore', and an atmospheric study of a door, slightly ajar, which they had entitled 'The Passage of Time'. (To the end of his life, any note I received from Ivan would be 'signed' with the scribbled outline of a cowled figure which I knew to be "ye olde Abbot Theodore".)

I had my first ever photograph taken with a bus. The photographer was Harry's friend, Ivan, and the bus was

AVF 351 (HLG 9)

which had bodywork slightly different from others in the same batch. The original body had been badly damaged on 30th July 1940 in an early morning air raid on the Bus Station, which had also torn apart AH 187. The bombs were dropped by a lone Dornier 215 at 6.00am. Some subtly-different brickwork in the Bus Station marked the spot. Many years later, I would conduct the funerals of both these men who were kind to me when I was young. I would not find them easy appointments.

Many of the old LLs (and the LJs, which had by then been painted red, and relegated to stage carriage duties) had roller blinds fitted in the mid-1950s. These, for me, destroyed for ever the flowing integrity of their outline. Not long afterwards the destination apertures were altered on most

62. This is the bus I first 'drove'. HPW 97 (LKH 97) went new to London Transport in January 1949, and was pictured passing Thorpe Station, Norwich on Service 92 soon after its delayed delivery to Eastern Counties one year later. (W J Haynes)

63. Here I am in that first picture of me with a bus, AVF 351 (HLG 9), when I was clerk to the Depot Mechanical Superintendent. This vehicle last ran on 14th February 1957. (Ivan Ames)

64. Ivan Ames's nom-de-plume:

Ye Olde Abbot Theodore

of the LKHs and the post-war LLs. Again, to me this was an aesthetic disaster. They never looked 'right' again.

Clearly, none of this mattered to the Company, and I'm certain it didn't matter to the public. So, why did it matter to me? Was my 'spiritual eye' fixed upon some mystical and unspoken ideal which transcended Company and passengers alike, making them mere instruments in the revelation of a greater truth? These are either deep waters or muddy little puddles of meaninglessness.

I believe the former. To the last days of my employment, nothing grieved me more than any perception that the Company was departing from its own high standards, and that history, custom, and practice could be set aside casually by people who didn't know, didn't care, and didn't understand. The present never exists in a vacuum. Without that corpus of tradition, there *is* no meaningful present - only perpetual, rootless, unsatisfying new beginnings.

Those ten months at Surrey Street were among the happiest I can recall. During the strike in 1957, I sat for hours in the ex-Beeston of East Bergholt Maudslay coach

LRT 133 (MS 907)

reading, and consciously enjoying the warmth of the brown leather upholstery (unusual for an Eastern Counties bus). Then I was given a pine disinfectant spray, and instructed to freshen every vehicle.

As an employee of the Company, and as I became known, I was able to obtain much information from other employees of varying ages. A few precious photographs began to surface, too. Reggie Brooks was retired, but put in a few hours' work each morning on small and menial duties. He shuffled round the garage with a hand-trolley collecting the clicker-boards which had been left scattered about, and returned them to their rack. One morning, he produced from his wallet the first photograph I had ever seen of a Norwich Tramways open-topped Guy double-decker at Mile Cross, with himself as the conductor. This precious item he allowed me to borrow and copy. (The span of my connection with the Company can be gauged by the fact that I was later to conduct the funeral of his son, Billy, for many years an Eastern Counties driver.)

The senior tours drivers, Freddie Harwood and Bert Vurley, belonged to United's pioneering days. In their long white coats, they were great men, and their bearing indicated that they knew it. In those days I didn't dare approach them. Their status was acknowledged even in the capital where the landlady of the boarding-house in Victoria, used by drivers on overnight shifts, afforded them the best bedroom, took them tea in bed, and ensured they sat at the head of the table at breakfast.

As a teenager with, as yet, no tales to tell, I loved the endless fund of stories: not just the dramatic ones, but the anecdotes which managed to convey something of the ethos of the industry. Wally Clapham's tale of bringing KD1 out of King's Lynn with over eighty passengers crammed aboard, during the war; and, from the same era, Ronnie Margitson and Jackie Hipper, then young apprentice-boys, driving the little Dennis 'Pigs' round the garage as soon as Ernie Kett, the Superintendent (Alec's predecessor), had gone to dinner....

But amid the entertaining and educating encounters came another Epiphany of overwhelming proportions. An inspector close to retirement was Tom Phillips. Learning of my interest, he drew from his pocket, without warning, a document which left me open-mouthed! Before me were full details of all the Tramways buses. Tom had worked for Norwich Electric Tramways Company, and his notebook recorded not only fleet and registration numbers but even the dates of delivery. It was a window into pre-history.

Information from a notebook thirty years old was, to a teenage enthusiast, stunning to behold. (Today I have records far older - but I don't carry them round in my pocket.) Here is a list of the Norwich Electric Tramways buses which did not survive to enter the fleet of Eastern Counties. These are runes of great power:-

CL 7478 (1) sd 1925 Guy. United body.
CL 7479 (2)
CL 7480 (3)
CL 7970 (4)
CL 7984 (5)

65. In its day, this style of Gurney Nutting body made its mark and was instantly recognisable. Here it was on the Maudslay Marathon III LRT 133 (MS 907), ordered by Beeston's of East Bergholt but delivered in 1951 to Eastern Counties who in the meantime had purchased that business. East Bergholt, Suffolk, was the birthplace of painter John Constable in 1776. The photograph was taken at Main Works and the other coach was Bedford EX 6557 (BS 922) in the Metropolitan livery it retained until after the 1953 summer season. (Roger Harrison)

66. One of the vehicles driven round the garage by the apprentices when the foreman went home for dinner was CAH 927 (D 7), a 1938 Dennis Ace 'Flying Pig' 20-seater shown here with female engineering staff during the war.

CL 7985 (6)
CL 8299 (7) sd 1926 Guy.
CL 8300 (8)
CL 9123 (9) dd 1926 Guy. Short Bros body.
CL 9124 (10)
CL 9125 (11)
CL 9126 (12)
VG 376 (13) sd 1928 Guy.
VG 377 (14)
VG 1468 (17) 20-seats 1929 Guy.
VG 1469 (18)
VG 1487 (19)
VG 2411 (20) 20-seats 1930 Dennis.
VG 2412 (21)

Each week at Surrey Street I pinned a 'Thought for the Week' on the notice board in one of the mess rooms.... I was given a photograph of some of the engineering staff; on the back had been written: 'JB's Disciples'.... I was young, inexperienced, and zealous. Yet my vigorous witness was respected. When I took my first ever solo Methodist preaching appointment at Salhouse (Sers. 33/33A), Teddy Palmer - a fitter on routine inspections - came, and brought his wife and children. Looking back, I can't help feeling that - in a totally unstructured manner - those Surrey Street engineers were the first people God gave me to care for.

It was too good to last. In the summer of 1957, I was transferred to Cremorne Lane and spent two interesting years discharging similar duties at Main Works. Where a few years earlier I had peeped surreptitiously through the wicket-door into a strange and exciting wonder-world, now I wandered freely at will, almost imperiously - into the mill, the spray shop (blinds), the trimming shop, the paint shop, the body shop, the pump room, and the dock. In my little white jacket, I squeezed between sign-writers, electricians, lathe operators, and fitters overhauling axles, engines, gearboxes, and ticket machines. I went into the forge, asked a question in the night-watchman's room, called at the stores, visited the buyer, Mr Brereton, Lenny Leverett, the typists - I was master of all I surveyed.

When vehicles arrived, new, from the coachworks, I inspected each one, and sniffed their newness; when buses came in with serious accident damage, I stood and stared and nodded sagely. Most of these activities were essential expressions of my responsibilities: a few were the excesses of the enthusiast. One of my friends, an apprentice, found a finger in the engine of

SAH 233 (LKD 233)

after a motor-cycling double fatality one Easter Day. At first I missed Surrey Street, with its operational frenzy; but Head Office and Main Works were the source of all authority. Job satisfaction remained high.

My small office was on stilts and squeezed between the offices of the Works Superintendent, on one side, and the Body Shop Superintendent on the other. It offered a panoramic view of the entire works, for these offices were set in the partition between the Engineering and Body Shops; a constant stream of chargehands and company officials passed before me - up the steps, past my desk, down the steps the other side.

Often, in pin-stripe suit and black homburg, the Chief Engineer himself would dash through, usually with an instruction or curt greeting, but rarely breaking his stride. Yet nothing in workshop or office escaped his eye as he passed, and his approach, or his unexpected appearance, or his command was never a matter of indifference. Senior management possessed style and gravitas in those days. J F Wood put my youthful illusions of command into perspective. He was the king - not me. I liked and secretly admired him. But he belonged to that exalted region which permitted no unbending before the lower ranks; there was no way a teenager could discover the man behind the phenomenon - which was a pity.

These were different men in a different age. Those were the days when the discreet exchange of a bottle of good malt at the Masonic Club would secure, in return, the operation of an excursion to

67. *'A few precious photographs began to surface....' This was one of the first, and created a lasting excitement. United AH 0521 (62) with Driver Furze and Conductor Fred Kingaby paused as it turned into Cucumber Lane, Brundall, in 1919. A particular fascination for the United enthusiast was the discovery of other photographs of the same bus in service in Northumberland. The task of getting it there from East Anglia on the rough dusty roads of the period defies imagination.*

68. *This is the Paint Shop section of the Body Shop in the Main Works in 1958. The tiny office of the clerk is in the centre between those of the Works Superintendent and Body Shop Superintendent. A small white jacket hangs behind his desk. The bus alongside is 1950 Bristol L5G KNG 711 (LL 711), nowadays preserved and restored to its former glory.*

Snetterton race track.

I walked up Cremorne Lane frequently on a variety of errands which took me back to Head Office, separated from Main Works only by a garden. I liked visiting the Wages Department where I had a soft spot for a pretty girl from Bunwell who came in to the city each morning on Service 27 (operated by an outstation AP class). Staff welfare queries took me to Peggy Sampson, who was the daughter of a former Secretary of the company (ex-ECRCC) and who remembered being lifted on to the counter, as a small child, by Jack Brereton at Ipswich. Peggy trained as a driver during the war. When her mother first saw her in uniform trousers, she said: "I always wanted a boy".

Best of all, I liked it when licensing matters entailed a visit to the office of Teddy Wormold and Cyril Green. (I didn't use their Christian names!) The former was bald and stout; the other had hair severely close-cropped. These visits were exciting, yet slightly overawing. Papers and files and timetables and leaflets and news-cuttings and mountains of fascinating paraphernalia were strewn everywhere. The office reeked with years of stale smoke, and the entire ambience was not merely old-world, but positively Dickensian. I thought I would have probably enjoyed working there - but the smell was horrible.

One outstanding memory of my time at Main Works concerns the events of Tuesday 25th February 1958. Snow had fallen overnight - but no great quantity. However, strong winds caused severe drifting and, throughout the morning, more and more buses on county services became stuck. The usual teams of fitters from Surrey Street were soon expended, and groups were despatched from Main Works to dig out and recover these vehicles. By early afternoon (as requests for assistance continued to arrive from Surrey Street) it was becoming more difficult to recruit further volunteers. It was then, to my boundless and inexpressible delight (and as proof of the management's desperation) I managed to get myself included in a gang sent to recover a familiar and well-liked vehicle,

UNG 177 (LKD 177)

which was stuck on Hart's Hill between Horsford 'Crown' and 'The Firs', not far out of the city, on Service 10. I was afraid it might be gone by the time we got there, but I needn't have worried....

A cruel and biting wind was blowing the fine snow off the aerodrome, and it stung wherever it hit. I remember a party of office-girls crying as they struggled past, walking home to Horsford. We worked hard, but I think our efforts might have been in vain if a snow-plough had not appeared and, with a tow-chain, given our bus that one, all-important jerk which freed it finally from the snow that had entombed it.

I returned to Main Works in X 31, the Works' lorry, arriving about eight o'clock in the evening, cold, hungry, exhausted, soaked - and exhilarated. At a different, practical, physical level - I had been *involved*. These endeavours earned me an additional 9s 7d (less than 50p!) overtime payment in my wages the following week. (I understand those three hours would now result in a flat-rate payment of about £15 which, like the 9s 7d in 1958, would post about 38 first-class letters.)

My 1958 diary has survived intact, and includes a few entries which acquire added meaning when juxtaposed with events (of which I learned later) in the city of brightly-coloured buses and trams. One date was particularly interesting in its implications. On Saturday 14th June I cycled to the manse and informed my minister of my decision to offer as a candidate for the Methodist ministry. (The manse was at 192, Thorpe Road, almost facing Head Office. It was, in addition, only a few yards short of facing 'The Redan', where the Thorpe Road trams had terminated.) In Glasgow, this was the last day that trams were operating on the No.7 route from Bellahouston to Millerston. Five years would pass before those names became meaningful to me.

On Friday 14th November I sent a postal order to R B Parr in Yorkshire for thirty photographs of Norwich trams, at 7d each. Most were by M J O'Connor. This was the last day that the No.12 trams from Mount Florida operated beyond Paisley Road Toll, along Govan Road to Linthouse and Shieldhall. The next day, I visited friends at their farm (which lay between the routes of Services 7B and 33A) and drove the tractor, carting sugar beet from the field. In Glasgow, the remaining (and principal) section of the No.12 route (Mount Florida - Admiral Street) was withdrawn.

69. *The journey should have taken an hour, but it took all day, and this picture demonstrates why. When two-year-old Bristol Lodekka UNG 177 (LKD 177) became trapped in a snowdrift on Service 10 on 25th February 1958, the first job was to rescue the passengers. I then took part in the Herculean efforts which eventually released the bus. (Eastern Daily Press)*

70. *Busy Glasgow tram Service 7 was flourishing when this photograph was taken by Bob Parr on 7th August 1954. It shows 'Cunarder' 1356 and 'Standard' car 71 at the foot of Golspie Street in Govan. The service last ran on 14th June 1958 and was replaced by the 106 trolleybuses the next day. (National Tramway Museum)*

On the morning of Sunday 16th November I conducted the first of my 'trial services' (part of a long candidating process) at Heartsease Lane Methodist Church, on the (by now, extended) Service 92. This was also the first day of the new single-decker trolleybus Service 108, on the Mount Florida - Admiral Street section. The bus stop was directly opposite Admiral Street Methodist Church.

I remember being so nervous in the pulpit at Heartsease Lane I could feel my knees buckling - an experience which, fortunately, I have known only seldom. It was important that I did well. If I had failed, I would never have preached at Admiral Street. But, again, I'm moving backwards and forwards at the same time…

Early in 1959 I witnessed the wonder of buses being born again. Three green double-deckers arrived at Main Works, having been purchased from Bristol Omnibus Co Ltd (where, I supposed, they had been replaced by Lodekkas). They went on the dock for major overhaul, then into the paint shop, emerging as three bright and distinctive additions to the fleet, everything made new:

FHT 801 (C 3235) (LKH 25)
FHT 806 (C 3240) (LKH 26)
FHT 808 (C 3242) (LKH 27).

On Saturday 28th February 1959 I went to Sheffield on

PVF 757 (LS 757)

(calling first at Marlingford 'Bell' to pick up Lenny Leverett and additional refreshment). We went to watch the thrilling FA Cup tie between Sheffield United and Norwich City. This was the sad day on which the Midland & Great Northern railway line closed. For me, however, the day contained additional excitement, unplanned and unexpected. Arriving in the city in good time, before the game my girlfriend (now wife) and I managed to squeeze in one tram ride through the narrow, industrial streets of Neepsend and out along Penistone Road to Wadsley Bridge and back. The spell was cast again.

Pype Hayes (and my last tram ride) seemed an eternity away. Then I was 13; now I was 19. And momentous events were afoot. My pilgrimage of exploration, from observer to employee, was about to come to an end. I had no desire to leave. I continued to be absolutely absorbed in my Eastern Counties world, which had enriched and equipped and enabled. But the train of events set in motion at Kelvin Hall was gathering its own, parallel, momentum. I filled in my 'Notification of Termination of Employment' form with a heavy heart but with the conviction that I could do no other. I had been accepted for training for the Methodist ministry. On Friday 31st July 1959, in a packed canteen at Main Works, I was presented with a Methodist Hymn Book and a Bible with the inscription: 'Preach peace to those that are afar off, and to them that are nigh'. I made a long speech, and was given a rousing farewell. I had become, again, an outsider looking in.

Later, I met J F Wood, who warned me against pomposity! Society, he explained, entrusted a degree of authority to policemen, schoolteachers, and parsons: but when they let it go to their heads and became over-officious and pompous, they were diminished and their labours counter-productive. It was our longest conversation: but I've remembered it, and tried not to be too pompous!

The next day I began two weeks' holiday at Willersley Castle, Cromford, in Derbyshire, from which two transport memories linger. On 6th August 1959 I photographed from a bridge the St Pancras - Manchester express, 'The Palatine,' double-headed at Whatstandwell. I'm afraid the result was not a prize-winning print but it was still mine, and the only railway photograph I had ever taken, and it was important to me.

More significant - though, at the time, interesting rather than dramatic - was an incident which occurred one afternoon as we returned to Cromford after an excursion. The coach stopped in Crich and our guide pointed and explained that the quarry on our right was to become a tramway museum. I stared, expecting to see a line-up equal to the vision, which still haunted, of Bird's yard at Stratford-upon-Avon, six years earlier - but, this time, in a context of hope. I saw nothing - but experienced a sensation of reassurance and approval. This was good news. Something was being done. But still I must visit that distant city of cream, orange and green buses, where trams still flourished and (I assumed) always would - or, at least, would for many, many years to come....

71. The 1949 body on the 1939 Bristol K5G chassis of FHT 801 (LKH 25), like its two companions, had been built by (what was then) Bristol Tramways. It was broadly similar to, yet clearly distinct from, the standard Eastern Coach Works body with which I was more familiar. In this picture, the bus is in St Giles' Street, pulling away from the City Hall stop.

72. The Sheffield tram ride is commemorated by this view of car 210 leaving Fitzalan Square for Wadsley Bridge on 18th March 1959. The kerbside loading stance, as in Birmingham, was one of a number of such features which showed that some of the problems which many people associated with trams could be overcome quite simply. (Philip Battersby)

73. In my student days between 1959 and 1963 the typical Birmingham bus looked like this, the designs of the various manufacturers taking second place to the distinctive Birmingham style. This one is 1953 Guy Arab JOJ 977 (2977) with Metro-Cammell body, the Corporation being very loyal to the local workforce in its choice of suppliers. The photograph was taken on 18th April 1967 in Harborne Park Road. (Philip Battersby)

12. The Birmingham student

But other pressures and priorities were claiming precedence. As a result of what had begun in the Kelvin Hall, the church sent me to Handsworth College, Birmingham, to commence four years of theological training. So, back I went, to the city where I had experienced those first dream-like, mystical, magical rides in 1953; back to the blue of Birmingham Corporation, and to Midland Red.

From college, our bus route into town was the Service 70 from Oxhill Road (Sandwell Road) which we boarded at 'The Grove', in what was still referred to as 'the village' and where, also, the Service 11 (the Outer Circle) - having turned right out of Rookery Road - headed off to Perry Barr. Service 70, which was operated, of course, by double-deckers and crews, had replaced the number 26 tram route six months before I was born! From Colmore Row (Snow Hill Station - one of the breathtaking discoveries of 1953) the Service 70 left town along Great Hampton Street, passed Hockley depot (trams until 1939), ran through Hockley Brook, passed the end of Villa Road and continued out along Soho Road - a route steeped in tramway history, and which (to me) still cried aloud for trams. Service 70 turned right into Grove Lane in which, also, trams would still have fitted admirably, and skirted Handsworth Park (as the trams had done, twenty years before). I enjoyed trips into town.

In addition to these journeys (and other midweek activities which necessitated bus rides) students were planned to conduct Sunday services over a wide area of the West Midlands and beyond.

My first public appearance in a dog-collar was on Sunday 20th September 1959. I travelled by bus to Snow Hill (the conductor called me 'Father', and declined to accept my fare), then caught the train to Stratford-upon-Avon, where I was met and taken by car to the village of Braires, three miles east of Shipston - on - Stour. There I conducted morning and evening services at the Methodist chapel. It was nearly ten o'clock before I arrived back at Handsworth.

The next Sunday evening I caught a Midland Red bus to Old Hill, for a Harvest Festival service. Over the years that followed I became well-acquainted with the buses of Birmingham and the Black Country. In addition, two spells of practical experience provided an unexpected bonus. In the late autumn of 1962 I spent a month at Ashbourne and renewed acquaintance with Trent.

In the spring of 1963 I was sent for a month to the Manchester and Salford Mission. Regularly, from Northern Moor I caught the Manchester Corporation Service 50 as it came, from Brooklands, along Sale Road and proceeded along Palatine Road through Northenden and

74. *Before setting off for Leeds on 27th June 1960 aboard United's Leyland Royal Tiger coach PHN 801 (LUT 1), I took its photograph. Here it is, appropriately sharing its stand in Surrey Street Bus Station with Service 34 to King's Lynn, where the coach would call en route to Newcastle on the service worked jointly with Eastern Counties.*

West Didsbury, past Lapwing Lane, on to Withington and Rusholme, passing the end of Platt Lane, and entering the city centre along Oxford Road. The Service 50 terminated at Piccadilly, which was only a few steps from my usual destination: the Central Hall, in Oldham Street.

College life has a lighter side, even for theological students. On Monday 8th February 1960 a coach-load of us travelled to our sister institution at Leeds - Headingley College - for a football match. Our route took us through Sheffield, where I was delighted to see the trams again (although, this time, there was no opportunity for even a short ride). I was especially thrilled to see them on our return journey, after dark, with the one centre-headlight preceding a sea of light. Trams at night were a new - and so fleeting! - experience.

On the same day, however, other hopes were raised in a tantalising but, ultimately, disappointing fashion. I noticed tramlines in Leeds, and my heart leapt, and I hoped against hope that - but, no! The last Leeds tram had run on 7th November 1959. I had missed seeing trams in Leeds by three months.

A close college friend (Revd David W Smith) was an enthusiastic officer in the Boys' Brigade. He gave hilarious accounts of the day - ten years earlier - when, as drum-major leading a parade of five hundred marching boys in Leicester, he threw the mace into the air enthusiastically but imprudently, for it landed and balanced on the tram wires at Humberstone Gate. The parade marked time while the mace wobbled and swayed before, at last, returning to earth.

At the end of my first year, I took a friend to see my college: but I insisted on making a detour. On Monday 27th June 1960 we caught a United coach from Norwich to Leeds:

PHN 801 (LUT 1).

This was the only occasion in my life when I *travelled* on a United vehicle. We looked quickly at two famous chapels - Brunswick and Oxford Place - before catching a bus to Sheffield.

Early next morning, despite the rain and a full programme, I managed another tram ride: along the Wicker and out along Attercliffe Road, Attercliffe Common and Sheffield Road to Vulcan Road. There, from the top deck, alongside Hadfield's famous steelworks where tram track had been manufactured, I photographed the car behind - 68 - as it arrived at the terminus. Again, my photo-quality leaves everything to be desired; the camera was not

75. Trams on a wet morning in an industrial city whose achievements span the world - Sheffield 68 in Vulcan Road beside Hadfield's steel works on 28th June 1960.

mine, and the morning wet and dismal. But memories are often fragmentary, hazy, and incomplete - like my picture; and I treasure it.

We caught a bus to Chesterfield - where East Midland still sported their strange, historic colours - then by other buses via Matlock and Derby to Birmingham. On Thursday morning, 30th June 1960, we travelled to London (Victoria Coach Station) at 80mph on the new Midland Red Motorway Express, returning to Norwich by train.

But here a sombre element enters my narrative. With three quarters of my college course completed, and immersed in church and family concerns, I was caught off-guard. The world doesn't stand still. During the last week of August 1962 I was reading a newspaper when I noticed a short item, merely one paragraph, stating that the once-famous Glasgow tramway system was to close. Only one route remained - the No.9 from Dalmuir West to Auchenshuggle - and it would cease to operate on Saturday.

I can still feel the sense of shock and bitter disappointment. Again, in theory, there was still time to stop everything and dash to Glasgow. In practice, the possibility didn't exist: prior commitments were absolute, and they prevailed. I was 22, married, penniless, a student grateful for vac-work, and 370 miles from Argyle Street. Now I would never see them - still less ride on a Coronation. I was vexed with myself for not making the effort, despite my commitments, to keep up-to-date. What a fool I'd been! The knowledge only intensified my sadness.

76. Conductor Frank O'Neill at Pollok on Service 50 early in 1964, shortly before he entered the driving school, and the author as minister of Govan Methodist Church.

13. Bellahouston-Govan-Gorbals-Bridgeton-Millerston

Less than a year later, I completed my college course, and the church sent me - to Glasgow. Sometimes, Divine timing leaves much to be desired. From 1963-65 I was minister of Govan Methodist Church, in Elder Street. The No.7 trams had been gone for five years, but the Service 106 trolleybuses provided a measure of consolation. The bedroom of our flat at the church, and the vestry (which doubled as my office) both faced the street. The flash from the overhead wires and the swift, whining rumble as the trolleys sped past the church became timeless symbolic memories of my short stay in Glasgow. Today, from the opposite end of my career, I look back to those seven hundred days as the most vibrant experience of my life. Only one thing more was needful.... (although the discovery of Barr's Irn-Bru provided some comfort).

After christening his daughter (and, later, his son) I became friends with Frank O'Neill, who stayed nearby in Greenfield Street and drove the trolleys, working out of Govan garage. Frank was two months younger than me. Occasionally, if I became bored with interminable sermon-preparation and endless study - and knew that Frank was on a late shift (or 'back shift', as they were known) - I would go with him for a ride to Millerston and back.

What a long, wonderful route it was! As the trolley came from Bellahouston I was picked up in Elder Street. The grey, tenement buildings which characterised this part of Govan (and, indeed, much of the route) have long been swept away. We turned right into Langlands Road, and first left into Golspie Street, passing the Salvation Army Citadel - home to the famous Govan band. (When the band visited Norwich Citadel at Easter 1987 I went to hear it.)

At the foot of Golspie Street the wires led right on to Govan Road, passing the Old Govan Arms bar on the corner. Now the long journey from west to east began in earnest. After passing the Lyceum, Govan Old Parish Church (with its pre-Christian site and sixth-century sarcophagus of its founder St Constantine), and the Pearce Institute on the left, and St Anthony's RC Church and Helen Street on the right, Govan Cross was reached (where Water Row led down to Govan ferry).

Immediately, beyond Govan Cross, railway lines crossed the road, leading from the goods station into the shipyard. On the right was the Plaza cinema and the handsome bank, with its pepper-pot top, at the corner of Broomloan Road (or Wine Alley!). On the left was Harland and Wolff's. A long, straight stretch of Govan Road led to the Prince's Dock and views of ocean-going ships.

The road skirted the dock (which had caused its realignment when construction work began in 1890) first bending right and passing Elphinstone Street, Vicarfield Street, Merryland Street, and Summertown Road (with South Govan Town Hall on the corner), before bending left into the long straight section of road with its magnificent row of tall cranes beside the South Basin.

Govan bus depot, Lorne School, and the Salvation Army hostel were at the end of this stretch of Govan Road, where the road bent sharply again to the left before completing its route around the Prince's Dock by bending sharply right and resuming its original alignment for the stretch down to Paisley Road Toll, where Paisley Road West joined it from the right.

A few yards further, also on the right, was Admiral Street, where - just inside - single-decker trolleybuses could be seen, and a Methodist church - the larger of the two in my circuit - where I preached regularly. Five years earlier, here would have stood the No.12 tramcars.

Beyond the Toll, the trolleys continued eastward along Paisley Road before forking right into Morrison Street and immediately passed the impressive offices of the Scottish Co-operative Wholesale Society, on the right. Morrison Street became Nelson Street, which passed under the bridge carrying the railway lines into Central Station and then became Norfolk Street (which pleased me, though by now we were in the heart of the Gorbals, where there was nothing else to remind me, even remotely, of Eastern Counties territory).

Where Norfolk Street cut across Gorbals Street, realigned itself slightly to the right and became Ballater Street, was Gorbals Cross. (The Cross itself - demolished before the Second World War - is lamented and described graphically by Ralph Glasser in *Growing up in The Gorbals*.)

Ballater Street led to the King's Bridge over the River Clyde, after which King's Drive (across Glasgow Green), and then James Street, brought us to Bridgeton Cross, scene of many a lively political gathering in former years. Here, at the heart of Glasgow's East End, the trolleybus turned left, briefly, into London Road, as if heading for the city, then right into Abercromby Street. By now, Elder Street and sermon preparation seemed far away. I had, again, been taken up in a chariot, and transported to other worlds and distant places.

Bellgrove Street, Duke Street, and Cumbernauld Road led out to Riddrie and to Millerston. At the terminus there was time for a chat and a joke. Then, as with every bus journey, we turned round and came back again!

I found the following entry in my diary for Thursday 24th September 1964:

'Coming back down Abercromby Street towards Bridgeton Cross, we met a trolley going east on which Eddie was the conductor. The buses stopped. Frank shouted out: "Jack's upstairs!" and Eddie shouted and waved in greeting.' (Eddie was a conductor I had met on earlier trips with Frank.) For a split-second, I felt involved again. It was a good feeling.

The 106 offered a ride to lift the spirit - a journey throughout which I dared not take my eyes from the window for a second, gripped by the fear of missing something: and I didn't want to miss anything. I wanted to absorb everything I could of the life and energy of this great city which, warts and all, had captured me utterly.

It was at the Glasgow Museum of Transport, newly-housed in the former tram workshops at Coplawhill, that I set eyes, at last, upon Glasgow trams and gazed in reverent silence. I was filled with awe. But an element, hard to describe, intruded and contrived to mar the occasion. It was like dashing to see an elderly relative - and arriving too late to do other than view the body. And there were too many other mourners; and they were noisy and irreverent.

And I recalled the Fishergate experience. Part, only, of the Coplawhill premises housed the museum. The remaining section had been cleared but not renovated: and its powerful vibrancy - created over so many years - persisted in a form almost tangible. Again, I looked in; again, I looked in vain. Yet the potent atmosphere seemed to convey the lingering essence of former days in a manner more valid and efficacious than all the wonders presented so cleanly and clinically next door. You could sense trams. If trams have spirits - they were there!

On Sunday 15th August 1965, I was invited to preach in the evening at the large St John's

77. On the south side of the Clyde, the location still nowadays called Paisley Road Toll marked the eastern end of the Burgh of Govan prior to its absorption into Glasgow in 1912. Admiral Street Methodist Church, on the right in this picture, was in an adjacent street where, in addition, the regular 108 trolleybus service terminated, like tram service 12 before it. Tram 334 had been new in 1909 but after an accident was rebuilt with major structural changes in 1946, as seen here. (John Humphrey)

78. It is appropriate for your Norfolkman to include a picture of a Glasgow trolleybus in Norfolk Street on Service 106. This one was FYS803 (TB 42) on 8th June 1966, with a rather alarming list to the nearside which did not appear to hinder its progress. (Philip Battersby)

Methodist Church in Sauchiehall Street. I thought of all the trams that had passed its doors, in that most famous of thoroughfares. I sat in a pedestrianised Sauchiehall Street not long ago. Casually, I glanced up - and my eye lighted on a rosette. It was true! They *had* existed in the wild.

One evening in the Spring of 1964, a teenager innocently and accidentally stuck a fist through the plaster on the wall of the church hall, which adjoined the church itself, at Elder Street, Govan. It proved to be the second of two trivial incidents (not integral parts of this discussion) which would lead me to become a worker-priest and bus driver for thirty-five years. That night, nobody could have foreseen those far-reaching consequences. We laughed; then I locked up, and went to bed.

The hole revealed extensive dry-rot, the scale of which presented an almost insurmountable problem to a relatively small congregation. Closure looked a distinct possibility. What contribution could *I* make? How could *I* make a difference? Even prior to working in Glasgow, the idea of leading-from-the-front (like Alec Mortimer) as a 'worker-priest' had occurred to me, vaguely and, perhaps, romantically. Before my ministry proper had begun, I was already concerned for the Church's relevance to modern society, and the effectiveness of its outreach. In Norwich, a 'gang' of youngsters my wife and I befriended (who lived near the old Catton Grove terminus of the 7A) had taught me that their world was light years away from our traditional ecclesiastical ethos. (The manner of my introduction to that gang was the first of the seemingly inconsequential incidents which, ultimately, were to determine the course of my vocation.)

Suddenly, the idea seemed vague no longer. I could work, perhaps, at Frank O'Neill's garage; contribute my church stipend wholly to the restoration fund; set an example to my people; and be involved daily in the world of the non-churchgoer. Sadly, my suggestion did not commend itself to the Methodist authorities at higher levels. Indeed, my letter did not merit a reply. My appointment was for two years only, and I left in 1965. In the struggle before them Govan Methodists asked only for one assurance: that they would continue to be allocated their own minister. (The little church on the Service 106 must have represented one of the most challenging and promising mission opportunities facing British Methodism at that time.)

After just one year, that understanding was revoked and the minister withdrawn. When the news reached me in the Fens, I was devastated and disgusted - and helpless. I submitted my resignation from the ministry, then withdrew it. Deeply disillusioned, it was then I vowed I would seek permission to pursue a 'worker-priest' pattern of ministry, when my current three-year appointment ended.

14. Fenland worker priest

My three years (1965-68) as the minister at Littleport, in the Ely Methodist Circuit, placed me securely back in Eastern Counties territory (which covered the whole of East Anglia, Cambridgeshire, the Isle of Ely and the Soke of Peterborough). The contrast with Govan was almost unendurable.

Having abandoned the cream, green and orange (but surrounded once more by red buses - and a familiar numbering system), my life-long enthusiasm burned brightly. However, in all things my vocation continued to take precedence.

Two things, in particular, delighted me at this time (in addition to the arrival of a Fenland daughter to partner the first, Linda, who had been born in Glasgow's Southern General). The coming of the FLF class - half-cab, front-entrance, double-decker - could only be described, yet again, as a spiritual experience. I even took some photographs!

And I became friends with George Washington, a driver at Littleport outstation and the son of Bert Washington, who had sold his business to Eastern Counties in 1938. Buses were still garaged in the old sheds, and George lived in the big house next door. George Washington, amused at my interest, was generous in his reminiscences and souvenir gifts, and filled a gap in my understanding of which I had been barely aware: the perspective of the small, local operator.

The full story of my worker-priest ministry - from an ecclesiastical viewpoint and, indeed, also from that of an enthusiast - is not appropriate on this occasion. My present purpose is served

79. This was Govan Methodist Church, where my two-year appointment was to have such a dramatic impact upon my life. The building in Elder Street was at the corner of Harhill Street, and I lived in the section on its extreme left, immediately above the front nearside of the bus as you see it here. Trolleybus FYS 848 (TB 87) was travelling south along Elder Street heading for Bellahouston in 1963.

80. When I moved to the Fens in 1965 I became aware of a different kind of bus history. Washington of Littleport had operated a range of interesting vehicles over a period of sixteen years, from a 1922 Model T Ford to the luxurious 1936 Dennis Lancet / Willowbrook 'radio coach' which became Eastern Counties DL 4. By the time his business was acquired by Eastern Counties in January 1938 one of this pair of 1928 Star Flyers (EB 7677) had been sold, but the other (EB 7693) remained, although not operated by ECOC and sold immediately.

81. Here I am at the beginning of my bus driving career, at Soham outstation in 1968 with Bristol LS MAH 744 (LL 744). I took care not to obscure the number plate.

adequately by covering the ensuing thirty-five years in broad strokes, mentioning highlights and drawing conclusions.

I rejoined Eastern Counties in August 1968, and travelled from Ely to Cambridge each day on Service 109 to attend the driving school (which operated from Hills Road garage - the old Ortona depot), and obtained my PSV licence (badge no. FF 22621). The site of the garage is covered now by a modern block of solicitors' offices. I was trained by a well-known Cambridge driver, Bill Hughes, and passed by the Chief Driving Instructor, Bob Colman. I took my test in

OVF 230 (LKD 230).

After an absence of nine years, I was an 'insider' again. The only vacancy available in the Ely area was at Soham outstation, as a one-man operator. Thus I commenced work as a driver not on old United or Norwich Tramways routes but on former Ortona routes. Soham was a two-vehicle outstation: in addition to LL 744, to which I have referred, we were frequently allocated

OAH 750 (LS 750)

of which, hitherto, I had thought only as the first (numerically) of the exciting new 1953 coaches (replacing the LJs), and in Metropolitan livery, at Great Yarmouth. Now I was pumping it round the Fens - and LS 753, too - to such unlikely places as Pymore, Wicken, and Upware. There is a symmetry to many of life's experiences which, occasionally, can be very striking. Further illustrations, even more dramatic, are to come. Another vehicle allocated regularly to Soham was

3009 AH (LM 947),

a Bristol MW I had seen arrive new at Main Works on 9th January 1959, which had heavy steering

- the result of accident damage repairs.

At Cambridge, I met a charming old retired busman from whom I obtained not only my first glimpse of an Ortona Scott-Stirling, but what was, for me, one of the most exciting Eastern Counties photographic discoveries ever. Conductor Frank Matthews was standing in front of

ER 7114 (AC 60),

a 1927 Leyland of which many photographs existed in Ortona livery, as an elegant charabanc with a hood for inclement weather. But here it was in Eastern Counties livery on Service 150: Cambridge - Caxton Gibbet - St Neots - Bedford, with a clicker-board, which proved that it must have had a different body fitted - and which my records didn't show. Another Epiphany moment! AC 60 was scrapped in 1935.

This was a daring, exciting, and alarming period. I felt I had reclaimed responsibility for my own life - not from God, but from an institution I loved yet had begun to distrust. The popular songs of the time captured (what was, for me) the heady atmosphere of that

summer of '68. *Lily the Pink* was still on the juke-box - but its place in the charts had been taken by *Sunshine Girl* and *Little Arrows*. Once my initial inexperience and fear had been overcome, those six months at Soham were extremely happy - even more than I was capable of appreciating at the time. Three drivers, each in our twenties, and each willing to co-operate - the job doesn't come any better. The shifts allowed us to meet together for a fry-up in the local café each Friday lunchtime. We were a unit and, again, it felt good. Our depot was Ely, where the services operated from Market Street in the shadow of the great cathedral.

The Ely drivers included ex-Ortona veterans (who, then, had been youths) like Les Saunders, who produced photographs of himself with (allegedly)

ER 8555 (Q 51)

and (definitely)

ER 5303 (S 46),

and George Cropley, who had an exciting picture (on which he appeared) of the opening of Ely garage in 1928, with a line-up of vehicles I had hitherto expected to see only in my dreams. These were (with their subsequent Eastern Counties numbers):

ER 7106 (Q 56)
EB 5893 (DE 50)
FE 9094 (R 65)
ER 7109 (Q 58).

At Ely, I met the retired Depot Superintendent, Bill Ramsay, from whom I obtained some interesting Peterborough Traction photos, including a view of one of the ex-Barnsley and District Traction Company 1913 Leyland S8s at Werrington 'Cock', and a picture of the Eastern Counties staff at March depot in 1932, with glimpses of

FL 8377 (A 46)

FL 4755 (S 12)

FL 5663 (Q1).

Identification of the '6' in 'A 46' was not conclusive. Several years later, Charlie Crane (whose career I shall describe) showed me his copy of this photograph. It had been taken from an adjacent negative. A driver had relaxed his shoulder: the '6' was entirely visible.

My first 'scrape' was at Ten Mile Bank, where I hit the bridge while reversing an LM in the dark one Saturday night returning from King's Lynn on Service 37, and working a Littleport shift on overtime. My despondency, over that weekend, was absolute. Another abiding memory is of a Saturday night trip to St Ives on Service 125 in thick Fenland fog, while working an Ely shift. I saw next-to-nothing throughout the journey, and was never more relieved to get back to the garage safely - until my very last day on the road. But, of that, fortunately, I knew nothing; only impenetrable whiteness....

In Fenland the elements seep into the conscious mind in a manner unusually direct and powerful. (Any who doubt this should read Graham Swift's *Waterland*.) Earth, air, fire and water are never vague, poetical, or incidental concepts but the raw and obvious stuff of everyday life.

The flat, black, fertile soil; the stunning skyscapes; the wind rushing in from the North Sea with nothing to check its fury (and, sometimes, creating dust-storms); the fire of the sun, the stars, (and, occasionally, farmers' beacon-like bonfires); rivers moving purposefully to The Wash, with miles of dykes and drains holding back waters forever waiting to pounce and reclaim what is rightly theirs - from King's Lynn (Service 37) to Cambridge (Service 109), these were the Fenland facts of life.

In winter, to relieve the pressure on dykes and rivers already full to overflowing, sluices are open and miles of grazing-marsh are flooded. These waters spill over certain roads, and I can remember driving slowly through them one afternoon at Sutton Gault on Service 124, taking care not to ease up on the accelerator (and, thus, suck in the water)! It seemed primitive and primeval and rather exciting.

A late-afternoon workers' special from Chivers' factory at Histon to Ely via Stretham and Wicken with

AAH 616B (LFS 78)

as snow began to fall, will also never be forgotten.

Those long straight Fenland roads, edged with dykes and surrounded by sky, have known many dramatic accidents.

FL 8377 (AH 246)

mounted the grass verge, split a telegraph pole, and crashed into a dyke near Horseshoe Bridge on 26th January 1949 on the Spalding - Peterborough Service 333. A year later, on 25th February 1950, it left the road again while overtaking a lorry outside Crowland and plunged once more into the dyke.

On the same route, tragedy struck on 2nd January 1979 when

WVF 600S (LN 600)

ran into the rear of an articulated lorry that had broken down at Peak Hill, Cowbit. Driver Noel Laxton was trapped in tangled wreckage, and after seventy minutes died of his injuries. LN 600 had entered service in March 1978. It was withdrawn, and its shattered remains lay for a long time in Silver Road.

'When I come home, on the last bus from Ely, on a foggy night which makes the Fens look, in the darkness, not so very different from a century ago, there are often two or three Fenland youths returning from the cinema or youth club.... When the bus stops suddenly, somewhere near Stretham, and the youths get off and vanish, apparently into nowhere, I remember the old men who, in their time, walked home along dark, and far muddier paths, after the evening's batch of stories in the nearest inn.

83. One of the shining lights of the bus enthusiast world is Mike Sutcliffe, widely known as 'The Leyland Man', and meticulous restorer of eight solid-tyred early Leyland buses. Among them is HE 12, a 1913 Leyland S8 originally operated by Barnsley and District, predecessor of Yorkshire Traction. Several similar vehicles (HE 8, 9, 45, 47 and 48) were transferred to Peterborough Electric Traction, and this picture shows one of them, unfortunately not identified, at The Cock, Werrington, a small village now in effect absorbed into Peterborough.

84. When taken on 19th August 1978, this Peterborough view was a typical enthusiast photograph of a new bus. In the event, the ill-fated Leyland-National WVF 600S (LN 600) lasted less than a year. (Maurice Doggett)

85. Crews were always ready to be photographed with their bus. Here, a United crew from Great Yarmouth, Driver 'Cuffer' Brown and Conductor Harry Miller, pose with 1923 Daimler CB PW 101 outside The Star at Martham.

'Only in the darkness, and by a great stretch of the imagination, can one have even a faint picture of the Fens and their people as they used to be.' - Enid Porter, in her introduction to *More Tales from the Fens*, by W H Barrett (Routledge & Kegan Paul, London, 1964).

15. Crew driver

Early in 1969 I transferred to Norwich and had to serve an apprenticeship all over again. I was granted a very short period of (mostly unnecessary) route-learning, which included a shift with Harry London and his conductor. Harry typified the immediate post-war generation of busmen, many of whom were well-known faces about the city. I certainly remembered Harry very well - and, later, he let me copy a prized snap-shot of himself as a conductor standing with rebodied (May 1940) ex-Tramways AEC

MV 984 (KD 132),

and another of him as a newly-trained driver. Sixteen years later, I conducted Harry's funeral.

At Norwich (with a waiting-list for one-man operation) I had to switch to crew-work - and did so gladly. Crew-work with a half-cab double-decker was much to my liking, and conducive to elevated thought! (Indeed, I wrote a script for the television series 'The Light of Experience' entitled 'The cab is my cloister'. After the broadcast, the text was subsequently included in a selection of scripts published in a small book.)

Crew-work hinges on the relationship between driver and conductor. Of my regular conductors over the years, three worked longest with me. Keith Burton was young, tough, and popular, and it was largely through being 'Keith's driver' that I became recognised in a large garage. We thought the surname a coincidence; it looked good on the crew-list:

Burton J.   Burton K.

Only later we discovered that my great-great-great-grandfather, William Burton (baptised 26th March 1749 at Bradfield, near North Walsham (Service 9) and married on 8th January 1775 at Bardwell (Service 215A)), was our common ancestor; we were descended from two of his sons. Our

86. Roll forward 48 years and Driver Jack Burton and Conductor Keith Burton consult their duty board on Service 92 at Heartsease Estate, Norwich, in 1971, with MAH 320 (LKH 320) which was withdrawn later that year. (John Ray)

meeting had been a bigger coincidence than we realised. Working at a shared task can produce a bonding effect, and drivers and conductors often became good friends. When Keith was apprehensive about an extraction, we went in uniform to the dentist's together. It's what mates do. They also play tricks:

NAH 940 (LKH 340)

was the driver training bus and the cab had a removable back window. In 1970 I was driving through St Benedict's Street on service 81, enjoying my solitude when - to my horror - a hand grabbed my shoulder in an iron grip. Discovering the said window was loose and ill-fitting, Keith had given me the greatest fright of my life. When he left to train for the Parachute Regiment I missed him greatly.

I worked with Michael Lutkin until he was 21 and himself became a driver. I christened his son. In a new century, I am christening his grandchildren. With Tony Lovett I spent eight years, which is a long time to work closely with one individual. When - seeing the end of bus conductors approaching - he jumped before he was pushed (not wanting to drive), I experienced a sense of loss for which I was unprepared, and which never truly healed. To some, that may sound extravagant; but anyone who has known the camaraderie of working together, day and night, summer and winter, year after year, will understand.

One thing about Tony interested me keenly. He was a very good footballer (and I basked in his reflected glory). He was not a shy person, yet of a quiet disposition, as if slightly lacking in confidence. It might even have been humility; certainly, I found the quality creditable and attractive. But on the football pitch, everything changed. Instantly, he assumed command, shouted instructions, took responsibility, and displayed an unaccustomed air of complete authority. The pitch was his stage. It lasted for a short while after the game - during the inquest, at least - but soon began to fade as 'normal' life trickled back around him, and the window of the game closed - a window which had shed light on a dimension of his being normally unseen. He also accepted engagements as a DJ, and was good at that, too. It was as if he could only be himself when performing. At the time of writing, Tony is my daughter's postman.

Driver Arthur Bartle had married a girl from Indonesia. His death from cancer, at an early age, left her distraught. Her tiny mother, who spoke no English, dashed alone across the world to be with her. I was to conduct the funeral - and to help make the service as memorable as possible, I wanted someone to carry the processional cross. Tony was not a churchgoer, but in the end he relented. He donned a cassock and surplice and carried the cross with the assurance of a professional. For that act of courage - for Arthur, and for me, and before many of our workmates - I admired him greatly.

The incident I remember most vividly when working with Tony was the day, on Service 25, we ran into a swarm of bees. We had just left 'The Ratcatchers' at Eastgate and climbed the hill, heading for Norwich, when we were enshrouded in what seemed like a cloud of smoke. Suddenly, I heard a noise like that of hailstones bouncing off the bonnet and canopy of my LFS. Almost immediately I received three bells. The front upper deck windows were open, and bees had funnelled in. I could hear passengers descending the stairs as fast as possible! I remained steadfastly in the cab. Eventually, Tony crammed all the passengers into the lower deck, and we proceeded with caution. When we arrived at Surrey Street, the bees hung in a large cluster between the upstairs front windows. My conductor vanished rapidly, more willing to face the roughest centre-half than this army of apian invaders.

At Norwich (and although their days were numbered) I was in time to drive LKHs on Service 92. But the times were changing. Eastern Counties became part of the National Bus Company. Soon, all the traditional route numbers had been altered. I was astounded at the casual manner in which this was done - as if it were merely an administrative matter, and the historical and sociological aspects wholly incidental.

Yet generations had grown up with those numbers. They were fixed points of reference in the collective subconscious of the community. They could be amended but not abandoned, because people knew them, almost genetically, and understood them. This social dimension counted for nothing. There was total unawareness of a problem. As a result, I suspect thousands of people (myself included) never again acquired an instinctive, confident, and comprehensive knowledge of their local bus network. So it was also bad business.

One sunny rest day, I visited the country cottage of a friend at Brampton (Service 10B), and - to fetch a scythe - entered one of his several garden sheds. I was amazed to find that cracks in the wooden walls had been papered over with a beautiful set of early 1950s posters. I recognised them instantly, having admired them in the bus station booking office - where regularly I collected leaflets - and in Pickfords, which - had I but known - was housed in what had earlier been United House - the United's offices in Prince of Wales Road, at the corner of Cathedral Street, in Norwich. The posters illustrated different parts of Great Britain and advertised holiday tours. Their survival in such circumstances was little short of miraculous. I was given ready permission to retrieve them - a small feat of industrial archaeology which, hitherto, has gone unrecorded! These, too, adorn my attic study.

In 1972 and 1973 I served as our TGWU branch chairman. On the day that I stood on picket duty at Surrey Street Bus Station, my mind went back to the strike of 1957 when, as the office boy, I was not required to strike, but was the subject of good-natured abuse when I 'crossed' the picket line, not least from George Blyth, a former Tramways bus fitter, whose pit had been directly opposite my office door, and whose loud voice and caustic, sarcastic comments had made me very wary - until I came to know him better; then I liked him very much, although he teased and tormented me endlessly.

Some private hire duties, which I enjoyed immensely at this time, involved taking the choir of Norwich Cathedral to sing in other churches, including Peterborough Cathedral (where I thought about Peterborough Electric Traction); Loddon (the still-recognisable terminus of the Great Eastern Railway service from Norwich, which started on 29th August 1905 - I have a wonderful photograph of CL200 - and was taken over by United in 1920); and Lowestoft (where everything United began), for a Benjamin Britten concert, one moonlit night.

Contract work, too, had a distinctive flavour. The prison contract, for example, involved driving a coach through the narrow main gate of HM Prison, Norwich, reversing in the exercise yard, and taking prisoners under escort to various courts. One day I took prisoners to Ipswich and Felixstowe.

87. Here I am with my conductor Tony Lovett circa 1976. Our steed that day was 1964 Bristol FS5G CNG 288B (LFS 88), and we were at Hellesdon (Parkway).

88. Tony was not a churchman but, after much persuasion, he allowed himself to be bravely pressed into service to act as crucifer when I conducted the funeral of a colleague, Driver Arthur Bartle, at St Clement's Church, Norwich, on 23rd January 1980. (R S Norman)

1976 saw the publication of my *Transport of Delight*, (SCM Press), which featured on the cover a photograph of KNG 471D (FLF 471).

To launch the book, I drove a new double-decker NAH139P (VR176) - filled with invited guests - from the Bus Station and along part of the former Service 92 route (passing the house where I was born) and into The Close, where the speeches were made. This book marked one of the critical moments in my worker-priest ministry. I was gratified and encouraged by the reception it received. I was reminded afresh of how much people like buses - or *want* to like them! I was enheartened by the way in which this costly combination of the sacred ministry (without stipend) and bus driving seemed to make sense to lots of people.

89. This photograph was specially taken at Surrey Street bus station in 1976 for the cover of my forthcoming book "Transport of Delight", which to my pleasant surprise later won an award. The bus was a Bristol FLF6G which had been new in November 1966.

The book led to invitations to preach from pulpits I might otherwise never have entered, including the great parish churches of St Mary, Ely, and St Nicholas, Great Yarmouth. I was particularly honoured by the invitation to preach at the university church of Great St Mary, Cambridge, on 1st May 1977. The vicar suggested the title, 'On missing the bus', which enabled me to begin:

"It is a great pleasure to be back in Cambridge - not, alas, that I achieved academic distinction here, but because I passed my PSV test in these narrow streets and obtained my bus-driver's badge. The day I first attempted to negotiate a double-decker past the parked cars in Petty Cury will haunt me for the rest of my life!"

The vicar, the Revd. Stanley Booth-Clibborn, later became Bishop of Manchester, and remained a supporter and sympathiser.

Another pleasant diversion from normal duties was the Norwich City Tour - with live, spoken commentary - I was asked to provide during the summers of 1982 and 1983. With Norwich famous as the 'City of Churches', I was able to combine three of my passions in a choice blend of buses, religion, and local history.

On the City Tour, I was sometimes allocated one of the brand-new Plaxton-bodied Leyland Tigers, which were painted in a special white livery with a broad blue band, and used on the Norwich - London service. Some of these coaches passed eventually to United, including

EAH 887Y (LT 887)
(1414)

which I drove twice in August 1983. I wish I could have known at the time that I was at the wheel of what would become a United vehicle. But I know now.

Early one evening, an interesting conversation took place in a Norwich pub. A long shift had ended, at last. It had been a hot day, and I called into 'The White Lion', near Whitefriars Bridge, for refreshment I felt was not undeserved. He was there already: artist, school-teacher, seeker after truth, disciple of Gurdjieff, and gleeful mischief-maker! He made the opening move.

"There is very little difference between your preaching and your bus driving," he asserted. "They are similar expressions of the same psychological needs."

"What do you mean?" I demanded, slightly abashed and extremely suspicious.

90. Another Leyland Tiger coach was EAH 892Y (LT 892), with which I was standing at Bell Avenue beside the Old Cattle Market in 1983, only yards from the spot where the showman's bus ex-DE 9 had puzzled me so deeply, many years before. I was about to operate a Norwich city tour with commentary.

He drained his glass.

"What sort of chapels do you like preaching in best?"

"Big, old ones," I replied instantly, "with a gallery all the way round, and a high pulpit."

"And what sort of buses do you prefer driving?"

"Double-deckers - old ones, with a cab."

"There you are: chapel with gallery equals double-decker bus. You like being in the pulpit, you say? - better than being a sidesman or a member of the congregation?"

"Oh, yes! I hate listening to other people's sermons!"

"And you prefer driving a bus to - say - being the conductor?"

"Gosh, I couldn't stand that! I like to be in charge."

"Precisely! So, for 'pulpit' read 'cab'."

Hard look from me, but - unmoved - he continued.

"Tell me - how are congregations these days?"

"Pretty thin."

"You find this disappointing?"

"That's not quite the word, but - Yes! I would like my chapel packed, with the gallery full to overflowing. That, in itself, would create a powerful atmosphere - then I could hold them, and sway them."

He considered his empty glass.

"And the buses? - the numbers of passengers are still declining?"

"Apparently. My conductor probably wouldn't agree, but I'm happiest when our bus is crammed with people. I like a full standing load - seventy or eighty people on the bus, all under my control, their destination in my hands."

He gave me a curious look, half-sympathetic, half-pitying, as though my childlike simplicity made it all too easy. Then he delivered his verdict.

"Chapel equals bus; gallery equals double-decker; pulpit equals cab; good congregation equals full standing load. The significance of your determination to be either in the pulpit or in the cab I'll leave to some other time. That may not be so nice. But it's as well you've finished up on the buses, if only for a spell. Your grammar school education probably appeared to preclude your becoming a bus driver - which was obviously an infant fantasy." (This man is a wizard!) "Unlikely as it may have seemed to you, your pulpit activities became a substitute. Pity you've backed two losers. Both industries are in decline. Guinness, please!"

I glared, unsure how seriously to take him, unprepared for such ruthless (if light-hearted) analysis, when all I'd wanted was a quiet pint of bitter. "Cheek…." I thought, "he's grinning again… but, then, his glass is full; he can afford to grin. What a load of nonsense! There couldn't possibly be anything in it…. could there?"

Hamilton Wood was a well-known and respected Norwich character. I included this reminiscence in my address when, as Sheriff of Norwich, I conducted his funeral at the Rosary Cemetery, on 8th September 1988, and it was received gratefully with that glad murmur of collective recognition which indicates warm affection at an accurate portrayal. But I could still see the grin; and I still wondered about the unfinished part of the analysis, which may not have been so nice.

16. Let us now praise famous men

Some professions - the church and the law, for instance - are renowned for their humour and wit. Their members are, at once, the embodiment and the custodians of a living tradition, and memories and reminiscences are told and re-told like creeds and scripture readings, and rehearsed like church history, and added to, daily.

The humour of the bus industry, and its vibrant, distinctive ethos, are recognised less widely - which may seem surprising given that many of the essential raw materials are present, not least the general public, moving machines, and the weather. But bus drivers and conductors are less likely to give after-dinner speeches than bishops or lawyers. Moreover, bus-related humour is heavily inclined to be 'in-humour', and without a working knowledge of the industry, many of the nuances are inevitably diluted or lost.

One of the things which saddened me most during the latter years of my service with Eastern Counties was that, often, I found myself wondering if we were laughing so frequently or so heartily. It may just have been me getting old. And modern life has become, paradoxically, more regulated - more strict and stern and serious; things once 'got away with' (or not, as the case may be) can no longer be tolerated (or attempted). Worst of all, much of the old carefreeness has been replaced by forms of stress utterly unknown in days when, at the terminus, there was opportunity to change the screen, visit the toilet, exchange a few words, and wait for the departure time. Today, all too often - with tight running-times and modern traffic conditions - the one-person-operator is already late on arrival at the terminus. (Note that I've written OPO, not OMO. I never learnt to say it - but at least I've remembered to write it.) The point I am making is that this added stress is faced alone - where, once, any problems were faced together.

Yet if ever an industry ran on laughter and a vivid oral tradition, it was surely passenger road transport - trams and buses!

91. Freddy Harwood is the driver at the wheel of this hybrid United double-decker No. 142. The company had a substantial fleet of such vehicles, which combined ex-military AEC Y-type chassis with B-type bodies purchased from the London General Omnibus Company and set back on the chassis to accommodate extra seats behind the driver.

92. As Senior Tours Driver, Freddy Harwood (right) appears again, this time in 1956 in front of coaches SNG 765 (LS 765) and UNG 766 (LS 766), about to depart from Surrey Street on the Norfolk Farmers' Bowls Tour. No modern driver's career could have spanned greater changes than his. The other great stalwarts with him were Bert Vurley (left) and Ernie Kett, the Depot Mechanical Superintendent.

Bert Vurley joined United on 24th June 1920 as a conductor at Southwold, where he had been born in 1902. At the age of 16, while working as a builder's labourer, he had helped to build the first United garage at Southwold, cleaning second-hand bricks for the footings at 6d an hour. He became a driver in 1922.

Alan Lewis assembled the brief account of Bert Vurley's fascinating life entitled *My Life Behind the Wheel* (Vintage Roadscene Vol 13, No. 51, June 1997). Bert told hilarious tales of those early days, including the time he lost a side of bacon from the back of an old Dodson-bodied AEC taking a sharp bend between Acle Bridge and Billockby on Service 7. It shot out, and into the dyke beside the road, and was never seen again. (I lost a wheelchair from the back of an LKH in 1970. As I swung right into Wolfe Road on Service 92 after climbing the hill, it continued its independent progress along Quebec Road for no small distance. The coincidence that it belonged to my sister didn't help.)

On another occasion, Bert accepted a chest full of tea and decided to put it upstairs (on an old open-top double-decker). As luck would have it, a nail was sticking up through the floor. When the crew came to fetch and deliver it, they dragged it across the top deck and, as it was lifted, driver and conductor were showered with tea.

Herbert George Vurley retired in 1969. Shortly before he died, at the age of 89, he said to me: "I've got arthritis, and angina, and I can't see; and if I stand up quickly I get a speed wobble!" He was a frequent passenger on the Costessey bus, sometimes travelling into the city, more often going in the opposite direction, down to the village. As I drew up at the bus stop, he would unsmilingly pull out his pocket watch and study it. I was more afraid of censure from him than from any of the inspectors. Then, once aboard, the banter, fun, and laughter would begin.

I gave the address at Bert's funeral in St Edmund's Church, Costessey - at the terminus of the old Service 13A - on 16th September 1991, and he was buried in the churchyard there, overlooking the beautiful Wensum valley. The reference number of his burial plot amuses me: E 10. It sounds like a United bus! Bert would have chuckled at that.

I didn't know Freddy Harwood personally, but I worked with his son Kenny, a fitter at Main Works, who lent me photographs of his father, to copy. However, I discovered an interesting reference to Fred in the *Eastern Daily Press* for Saturday 16th November 1929.

'A number of motor drivers were summoned at Norwich Police-court yesterday .... for driving heavy motor cars at a speed of over 20 miles per hour on Newmarket Road.

'Police-sergeant Palmer said that with Police-constable Hook he timed various motor vehicles over the measured quarter of a mile on the Newmarket Road, between Eaton Road and a spot by Branksome Road....

'In the case of Frederick Herbert Harwood, of 21, St Stephen's Square, Police-sergeant Palmer stated that defendant was driving the London service United bus down Newmarket Road at about 7pm. It covered the quarter of a mile in 23 seconds, a speed of over 39 miles per hour. It overtook a car and two cyclists. No horn was sounded.

'Defendant said he had driven for the United Company since 1916, and had been on the London service ever since it started. The machine he was driving had highly efficient brakes, and was fitted with a governor which kept its speed below 35 miles per hour. He always dropped down to 20 miles per hour on Newmarket Road....

'Superintendent Christie said that there were five previous convictions against defendant for driving buses at a speed exceeding 20 mph, the last being in December, 1928, when he was fined £10.

'Mr P A Bainbridge, who defended, said that the United Bus Co considered Harwood to be one of their very finest drivers, and he had been doing most responsible work for them.

'The chairman said that the magistrates considered this a serious case, and it looked as if defendant had not learnt a lesson. He would be fined £4.'

Charles Crane's lifetime of service to the bus industry was crowned with the award of the BEM. At the time of his retirement, he was Chief Inspector for the Eastern Area, and later wrote a short memoir describing some of his experiences (many of which I heard recounted first-hand). The story of his 'call' to the bus industry had almost Biblical resonances.

93. In the years immediately after the First World War when Bert Vurley joined United, the company was expanding rapidly and making extensive use of somewhat unpromising equipment. This AEC charabanc is a case in point, and must have proved a challenge to the youthful Bert Vurley who is seen here at the wheel. The slightly forbidding characters behind him were perhaps a challenge of a different kind.

94. Bert was well into his retirement when he stood with me in front of 1977 Bristol VR TEX 407R (VR 197) at Surrey Street, but he had worked long enough to have experienced the near-miracle of the semi-automatic gearbox. Notice how carefully we left the numbers clear for you to read!

Young Charles worked at a book and newspaper stall on the green outside Horning 'Swan', where the 'Broads Service' 5, which ran between Norwich and Great Yarmouth, turned off the main road, dropped down into the village, and reversed outside 'The Swan', beside the river, before returning to the main road.

One morning (22nd June 1923) driver Harry Warren, a good customer, told Charles the United company was looking for conductors, and offered to recommend Charles if he cared to apply. On the return journey from Norwich, Harry told Charles he was to go for an interview that very morning! The youth was at his wits' end - then made his decision. Risking the wrath of his employer, he closed the bookstall, took his cycle over Horning ferry, and set off for Recorder Road. As he cycled, a vocation was born. Charles became more and more keen to get that job. And he did! Shades of 'Follow Me'.

Charles Crane worked as a conductor at Norwich and Acle, and became a driver in 1926. He was then based successively at Norwich, King's Lynn, Holbeach, back to King's Lynn, back to Norwich, then Sea Palling.

95. The boy who heard the call! A delightful photograph of young Charlie Crane with United AH 8736 (B 221), a 1922 Dennis acquired with the purchase of Norfolk Road Services Ltd, of King's Lynn, in 1926.

He became an inspector at Peterborough in 1934, superintendent at March in 1938, and Chief Inspector of the Western Area, based at Cambridge, after the war. One of his tasks was to wait in the yard and catch young George Washington tumbling out of bed at the last moment at his house beside the outstation at Littleport.

Charles Crane's knowledge of the entire Eastern Counties operating area was second to none, and his brief account did scant justice to the wealth of anecdote he possessed. His conductor-training commenced on 23rd June 1923, the day after his great decision, on Service 7A with a solid-tyred AEC open-topped double-decker. He went on to spend much of that summer on Service 10 (Norwich- Cromer).

"One night, on the way into Norwich, we stopped at Newton to place the carbide chamber into the water-container in order to 'light up'. My driver, to his dismay, found the container empty, as also were the side-lights of oil. Neither had been replenished earlier. We went across to 'The Crown' and bought some candles which were placed in the oil containers, and proceeded on our way to Norwich - but not before having a drink. I had never tasted beer before and did, in fact, ask the driver for ginger beer, but he must have misunderstood me...."

96. From Charlie Crane's wallet came this picture of PW 1938, one of the United 'chasers' on White chassis, photographed in Recorder Road, Norwich. Damage to the print has caused the loss of the top name from the destination board. At this date circa 1924 the 7B was newly introduced and extended as far as Blofield. Only later did it reach Pedham and Panxworth.

Charles Crane's story of the cat that vanished is another which typifies those (what were still) pioneering days. One afternoon in November 1923 Charles's bus was about to leave Norwich (outside Thorpe Station) at 4 o'clock on the Service 7 to Great Yarmouth when the parcel agent who kept the bookstall at Foundry Bridge brought him a large wicker basket containing a valuable cat and addressed to a private house in Newtown, Great Yarmouth.

Normally, livestock was not accepted, but Charles agreed to take it; there seemed no other way out. The skep was placed at the rear of the bus - a Norfolk saloon - with the other parcels. The bus had not progressed far when the cat managed to poke its head out of the basket. To save further trouble, Charles took it to the driver who put it in the locker underneath the front seats. Then they forgot it!

They proceeded to Yarmouth, returned to Norwich, then back to Acle for the night. The bus had been put in the outstation garage and the engine switched off - when a scuffling was heard. The cat! They opened the locker and out it leapt.

After much chasing round the garage, it was finally returned to the basket, and the lid secured with string. With the help of his driver, the skep - a foot high - was strapped to the carrier of his motor-bike, and Charles set his face again towards Great Yarmouth. A thirty-mile round journey lay ahead: to Newtown, back to Acle, and home to Rackheath.

He arrived at the address.... the string was unravelled.... the skep was empty! The cat had gone! The man of the house mounted his own motor-cycle and the two bikes retraced the journey to Acle - but no sign of the cat was ever found. To his relief - and surprise - Charles never heard anything more about the incident. Perhaps the cat found Bert Vurley's side of bacon....

The following year, Charles found himself regularly on Service 7B (running from outside Thorpe Station yard to Blofield 'Two Friends') and caught up in one of the characteristic features of the industry at that time: competition with the opposition. An American-built vehicle - a White - was used as a chaser. It was a very fast fourteen-seater which operated in front of the opposition and scooped up all the prospective passengers. Charles worked on both the service car (a Daimler saloon) and the chaser.

An article I discovered in the *Eastern Daily Press* of 14th October 1924 corroborated Charlie's account in every detail. It described how, at Blofield Petty Sessions, Reginald Alfred Creed, of Rose Yard, St Augustine's, Norwich, was summoned for driving a motor bus in a manner dangerous to the public at Thorpe St Andrew on September 18th. It was alleged that at about 10.30pm a motor bus belonging to Walter Kerrison Bambridge was proceeding from Blofield to Norwich. When it was on the Norwich side of the railway bridge - approaching the second curve, and facing Brooklyn Terrace - a United bus overtook it, with only inches to spare, and cut in sharply. The Bambridge bus - painted yellow, like some of the United buses - braked sharply and swerved on to the path, but could not avoid a collision, in which its off-side lamp was wrenched off and its headlight and mudguard damaged. It had been travelling at about 12 mph. Nothing had been coming in the opposite direction to force the United bus to cut in.

The driver of the Bambridge bus said he knew what the defendant's bus was, and he was always on the look out for it, as it was a fast one and was always cutting in. The United had been on the road five years. Mr. Bambridge himself, who had been acting as conductor on his own bus that night, said he was not unfriendly with the United drivers, but their company was trying to drive him off the road. He did not see the United bus door open until both buses came to a stop. Mr Bracey, for the defence, said that the defendant had a clean record for twelve years as a bus driver, and during the war was a driver in France.

Charles Arthur Crane, the conductor on the United bus, said they had passed the other bus when they drew to the side of the road to pick up a passenger. The opening of the bus door was recognised as a signal to any bus behind that they were stopping to pick up or let down. They were 20 yards in front when the passenger was picked up. The Bambridge bus ran into them.

The bench imposed a fine of £3 with £2 10s costs. W K Bambridge was eventually bought out by Eastern Counties in January 1934.

On my later visits to see Charlie in hospital, when he was as friendly as ever but slightly confused, I made a point of going in uniform. When he asked, "What road have you been on today, boy?" I always replied with the nearest relevant traditional route number - 92, perhaps, or 10 - not the literal, factual, modern, and (to him) meaningless one. Then his eyes would light up in recognition, and he would nod happily with understanding. I conducted the funeral of Charles Crane BEM, on 6th February 1991.

Teddy Barker was born at East Dereham in 1912. He joined United as a conductor at the age of 15 in 1927, travelling to Norwich to take the numeracy test at a separate little office United kept in Rose Lane. His first driver was Harry Robinson, their regular bus

PW 3333 (AA 230),

and their route was Service 13: East Dereham, Yaxham, Mattishall, East Tuddenham, and Costessey (where it diverted through the village, turning left down Longwater Lane, through the little ford - now a bridge - and back along Town House Road and Norwich Road).

I can recall Inspector Barker checking my Costessey bus, chatting earnestly with an elderly lady and requesting that we set her down at a precise point between stops. "You know where she gets off, don't you?" - a plain link, I suspected, with those former days. It was while he was working as a conductor on this route that he met his wife, Phyllis, whom I knew well; they were married for 62 years.

When he was 21, Ted had to go driving and passed his saloon test (i.e. single-decker) in a P-type. At first, he drove only at week-ends, as-and-when required. Young busmen were moved around by the Company in those days, especially on holiday relieving, in a way which would not be tolerated today. Ted went all over the county and, indeed, was at Cromer during the summer of 1935 for the whole season. One of his favourite recollections was of picking up the Revd Harold Davidson, Rector of Stiffkey, on Sunday evenings after evensong, and taking him from Blakeney to Norwich

97. Chief Inspector Crane was the proud custodian of FCL 147 (Y 93), a 1952 Austin A40.

98. The United F-class Associated Daimler of 1927 was in the red and white livery by the time of this photograph, which dates it to 1930-31. Conductor Teddy Barker, working on the Norwich - Dereham service, was obscuring the number plate - you had also to be an enthusiast if you were to learn not to do that! Note the 'United' cap badges worn by Teddy and his driver.

where he caught the late train to London. In a famous case in 1932, the rector was unfrocked before the high altar of Norwich Cathedral for immorality.

Ted's stories flowed endlessly. If only I had collected more of these memories, and on a wider and more systematic basis! What an important (and entertaining) social record they would have formed. But I didn't have the time. My agenda had been set on April 28th 1955. Other matters claimed priority. But I talked with Ted often, and noted this tale particularly because it involved one of my TD4s.

"I took the bus Jack Friend hit the Guildhall with to the coachworks at Lowestoft for repair. I had to go via Acle and Yarmouth because double-deckers weren't allowed in the street at Beccles. I touched sixty on the Acle Straight. It was lovely, beautiful! I can remember hearing the little bits of glass dropping on to the floor" (from the broken windows).

Teddy Barker had his audience in convulsions of laughter when he described how, on manoeuvres with the Army in the late 1930s, a party of drivers were tormented by insects, and he had to apply ointment to Wally Oxberry's mosquito bites. (Knowing, and being thus able to visualise, the individuals concerned made the tale all the better - except that we were picturing them as they had become, not as the young men they were at the time.)

Teddy Barker became an inspector in 1947. I knew him personally over forty years - but because he was such a familiar figure about the city, I cannot recall ever not knowing him, at least by sight. The inspectors of his generation could not be fooled easily. They knew all the tricks; they had invented most of them. Drivers often gave their conductor a quick, warning flash of the internal lights if an inspector was spotted. One conductor recalled: "Whenever Teddy jumped on, he always asked: 'Something wrong with your lights, conductor?' He always let you know he knew!"

Teddy Barker loved news and gossip. He was incredibly shrewd. He laughed and smiled often, and it was a mischievous, knowing smile - a Norfolk countryman's smile. In his old age I grew very fond of him. When I visited him he would recite 'Let not your heart be troubled; neither let it be afraid'. But he was not a churchgoer. Thinking of him again has moved me, even as I write. I conducted his funeral at the ancient Great Hospital church of St Helen's, Norwich, on 18th September 1998.

17. Cyril Harris

If, at Norwich, Freddie Harwood and Bert Vurley were the Archbishops, Cyril Harris was Bishop of London! Cyril's reminiscences, too, were not only continuous but often very funny. He was born on 12th April 1908 in Pietermaritzburg in South Africa, where his father was a company sergeant major in the 2nd Norfolks. As a baby, he had a short stay in Gibraltar, then sailed through the Suez Canal to India. He left India in 1916 in a troopship guarded by four warships and returned via the Cape. Coming through the Bay of Biscay he was "sick as a toad" and lay in bed for two days.

Thus Cyril was nearly nine before he reached Norwich, and didn't see his father again until after the war. Cyril's mother bought her groceries from Mr Dunham's shop at No.11, Rupert Street. Mr Dunham also operated a small fleet of buses, and Cyril's mother asked if her boy could have a job. Mr Dunham promised, "When he's seventeen I'll take him on". So Cyril had to take other jobs until 1925, when Mr Dunham kept his word.

Russell Charles Dunham owned the Central Bus Services, and operated his red buses from a garage in Mountergate opposite the Fish Market. 'The old man' (as Cyril referred to Mr Dunham to the end) sent him to the Watch Committee at the Guildhall and he was granted a conductor's licence.

He started work on the Watton run, on an old AEC 28-seater single-decker. George Adams was his driver, and as they were going along he taught Cyril to drive. There was a seat near the driver, and he let Cyril change gear; then he would sit to one side and say "You can drive now".

So Cyril was taught to drive in less than three weeks. George Adams said to the old man: "He can drive, now". So the old man gave Cyril a Model T Ford and sent him to the old tin hut on the Market Place (which served as the police station) and the sergeant took him out on test, which

99. 'The bus Jack Friend hit the Guildhall with' can be identified here as AAH 145 (AH 241), photographed on that occasion in March 1937. The other bus is an LG-class Bristol GO5G, possibly AVF 356 (LG 14), and the pair were on Norwich tramway replacement services 80 and 89 respectively. (George Swain)

100. Here is Russell Dunham's LF 8889, still with its embossed London General fleet number B 2281 on the bonnet, at the Red Lion, Drayton. This was the outer terminus, some four miles north-west of Norwich city centre, of the service which subsequently became United, and then Eastern Counties, 29A. The bus was licensed to Dunham in 1923 and 1924 at least, and the original postcard from which this picture is taken was posted on 11th June 1926.

included a hill start on St Matthew's Road (close to where the 92s would eventually run, and beside the church where I would be christened).

After that, Cyril was a driver. All the Central services started from All Saints Green, except the Drayton service, which started from Riverside. The regular vehicle on that run was an old ex-London General B-type, which Cyril sometimes drove. "The steering was so light that you could turn in the road almost with one finger," he recalled. It was probably

LF 8889 (B 2281).

He also drove the little Berliet, which had twin wheels at the back, fastened only by a type of split-pin which - when it wore - was prone to shear. Once, Cyril was at Little Melton - "near the parsonage" - when he heard something crack, the bus dropped to one side, and he watched two wheels go past!

When R C Dunham sold out to United on 1st June 1928, Cyril was one of the drivers who took five of the vehicles to a sale-yard at London. They slept that night in the buses, and charged United for their board.

After the takeover, the former Dunham garage in Mountergate was used by United for storage until it was destroyed by fire in the early hours of 15th October 1928. Two new single-deckers were burnt out - J 51 and J 113 - and three charabancs: E 27, E 28, and E 37. Percy Smith, the depot foreman at Recorder Road, lost his car; "but he got a new one out of it", Cyril assured me, adding "He later kept the 'The Free Trade Tavern' at the corner of Rose Lane and John Street".

Cyril worked out of Recorder Road, but as United expanded and as vehicles became larger, space was at a premium, and buses had to park elsewhere. "At night, after we had finished, we had to drive up to Mousehold aerodrome to fill up and garage in one of the old hangars. It was the second hangar - later used by Caley's Crackers." It was then that Cyril casually mentioned that, when the Corporation opened a new dustcart depot in Westwick Street, buses were also parked for a time in the old depot in Fishergate. I listened open-mouthed! This was a true Epiphany; and it was also a confirmation - for, somehow, I had known it, all along. (United vacated the Fishergate premises on 31st December 1929.)

Cyril Harris had a fund of wartime stories. After Dunkirk, about ten drivers and buses were allocated to various regiments. Cyril went with The Royal Berkshires, and his imitation of the officer correcting his pronunciation was priceless: "Rahl Barkshah…!" There were tales of parking-up in woods at Beachamwell; of Stanley Palmer soon looking like a tramp, and catching a rabbit; of Stanley being challenged by the sentry (who had been primed by the other drivers); of sleeping under the trees, and Stanley taking his teeth out in the night and of cattle moving about, with distasteful consequences for Stanley - the stories went on and on, in the time-honoured tradition of busmen.

After the war, Cyril switched to mainly coach work. He won the premier award in the 'Concours d'Elegance' section of the second British Coach Rally at Brighton in 1956, with

UNG 766 (LS 766).

That was the year I met him first. He was the natural successor, and equal in every way to men like Vurley and Harwood - a "drivers' driver", very popular, and the automatic choice for staff outings. He was the senior driver when he retired in 1973.

The stature of men like Cyril Harris and their place in the scheme of things was illustrated for me neatly in a trivial incident I noted in 1970. To run into Thorpe Station yard early was to invite a booking or stern warning from the inspector. It had happened to me, not long before. One day, I had just arrived at the station on Service 81 and climbed from the cab when the bus behind arrived. Knowing there was a senior inspector in attendance I watched with amusement and anticipation. It was Cyril, who had plainly done a round trip 'on the city' to help out. He hurried to catch the Service 90 single-decker, back to the Bus Station. He and the inspector chatted merrily; time-keeping didn't feature in their conversation. The 90 moved off, and Cyril was gone. He was under a different dispensation from me.

I conducted Cyril's funeral on 23rd January 1998. Teddy Barker was unwell, and I mentioned in my address how deeply he regretted he could not be present. Later, Cyril's daughter, Patricia, gave me his long-service gold watch. It remains a treasured possession.

101. Cyril Harris (centre) poses with four colleagues before one of the Bristol JO5G coaches new in July 1937.

102. Cyril Harris was the first-choice driver for works' outings by management and staff alike, and on this occasion when his off-duty colleagues were enthusiastically downing their beers, Cyril was discreetly holding the bottle in his hand and smiling at the camera. As for the LE-class coach, the lack of destination blinds suggests that it was new, which would date the occasion to 1949 or 1950.

103. The typical 1920s group photograph of a charabanc party rarely showed the bonnet and front of the vehicle, but in this case the machine is identified by the large fleet number '34', and the registration number is just about discernible on the original photograph. It is XB 8418, a 1920 Tilling-Stevens TS3 of the Eastern Counties Road Car Company. Jack Brereton, who had joined the company in 1919 - the year of its formation - is standing, fourth from right.

18. A noble line

Arthur (Bunny) Peck, born in 1910, joined Norwich Electric Tramways Company in 1926 as a parcels boy, and shortly afterwards became the points operator outside the Royal Hotel. I asked him if ever he'd sent a tram the wrong way. "Plenty of times!", he chuckled. Then the tram would have to reverse before continuing its journey.

Bunny Peck trained as a conductor on the Tramways buses in 1928, and became a driver in 1937. Quietly spoken, Bunny Peck was an enthusiastic union man, in which connection he served for many years on the Schedules Committee. In a note to me, outlining his career, he concluded: "I have had a very enjoyable and very happy life on public transport." While I sat at the wheel of my bus one day, he appeared at the door and asked me quietly if I would take his funeral when that day came. He had reached the age of 86 when I was called on to fulfil my promise, on Monday 13th January, 1997.

Jack Brereton's central role in this tale of enthusiasm has already been gratefully acknowledged. I spoke with him at length, again, in 1994, when he was aged 90, and found his reflections profoundly interesting and very moving:

"I was born in Ipswich on 12th November 1903 and won a scholarship to the secondary school. I left school in the summer of 1919 and hadn't a job to go to. I was living on London Road with my two brothers; father was working away much of the time, and mother had recently died of consumption. I went to the Labour Exchange and they gave me two introductory cards - one for Tollemache the brewers, and one for Eastern Counties.

"I thought Eastern Counties looked the most interesting so I decided to try for that. They'd then started running two buses between Ipswich and Felixstowe. The buses were red, open-topped double-deckers brought from the streets of Brighton, and still said 'Tilling' on the side. The company hadn't a garage in those days, but in Museum Street a veterinary surgeon named Mr Phillips had a tall building with a glass roof, and they parked the buses there. You can still identify the place - on the same side of the street as the chapel, and a little further up, towards the town.

"The Company's registered head-office was an ordinary house with the ground floor converted, at 32, Silent Street. It was there I went to be interviewed by Mr Joseph Worssam, the General Manager. He was pleasant, and I was given the job. I still have his letter confirming my appointment. Claud Sampson was the clerk; I was engaged as the junior clerk, and Miss Hamilton was the typist - the three of us ran the office. The Traffic Manager, Frederick Haynes, lived over the office and, eventually, his son came and worked in the office with me. Claud's small daughter, Peggy, was sometimes brought to the office, and I would lift her on to one of our high clerks' stools and give her a farthing.

"The company was expanding. Our buses ran from the Old Cattle Market - from the street in front of 'The Blue Coat Boy.' The early routes were Service 1 Felixstowe, Service 2 Shotley, Service 3 Woodbridge, Service 4 Stowmarket, and Service 5 Hadleigh. I have also preserved the pass which enabled me to travel free on the Hadleigh bus, which came in along London Road." (Subsequently - as I mentioned - both of the documents to which Jack referred he entrusted to me for safe-keeping - a solemn and thrilling charge to any enthusiast with a sense of history.)

104. I felt a particular sense of occasion in 1994 when I stood outside my home with Jack Brereton who was then aged ninety. I marked it by wearing a Norwich Electric Tramways cap badge, which had been a gift from the widow of the late Inspector Jack Sutton.

"I remember when United - who ran bus services in Norfolk and in the Lowestoft area - began operating in Ipswich. They were the opposition, and their grey buses ran (from St Margaret's Plain, I think) from Ipswich to Felixstowe. Eventually, an agreement was reached, and United withdrew from the Ipswich area. We ourselves had an outstation at Wisbech. I can remember sending a wages cheque there."

Jack had three stories dating from those days when Eastern Counties double-deckers were open-topped. His favourite interested me because it seemed to encapsulate a quality of gentle innocence soon to vanish for ever. A group of youths kept ringing the bell - which was not the modern press-button type, but a long cord - until, at last, the irate conductor silenced them by shouting "Can you play 'The Bluebells of Scotland' on that?!" I waited for the punch-line - but that was it! After seventy years, Jack Brereton would still laugh heartily at that memory - while I found his merriment more amusing than his tale.

105. Posing on the steps of the Market Cross at Wymondham are the officials and wives of the Engineering Department at Main Works, circa 1950. In the front row (with one standing behind) are Cyril Harris (left), Arthur Lay (6th from left), J F Wood (Chief Engineer, 8th from left), Monica and Jack Brereton (7th and 6th from right), J W Robson (3rd from right) and Charles Crane (right).

His other two reminiscences, however, would raise a smile in any age. A woman boarded the bus and went upstairs. After a while, she called out: "Will you stop at Number 107, please?" Ever willing to oblige, the bus stopped outside Number 107: but the woman didn't alight. Instead she held up her little dog and said: "That's where you were born, dear!" Another elderly woman boarded a bus one day and went upstairs, calling as she went "Wait a minute, young man!" She sat down on the top deck - then stood up, and came downstairs again. "Aren't you going?" asked the conductor. To his surprise, she replied: "I thought if I could manage the stairs, and it's fine, I might go tomorrow."

Jack continued his reflections. "The company continued to expand throughout the twenties. Workshops were built at Foundation Street, and we moved out of Silver Street to new offices situated at the corner of Lower Brook Street and Dog's Head Street, where a new garage had been built. It was there I met Monica, who worked in the enquiry office taking bookings for the London coaches.

"When the new company was formed in 1931, Mr Worssam became General Manager, and Mr Sampson the Secretary. I remained at Ipswich in charge of secretarial duties for a few months until, later in the year, all the remaining secretarial work was transferred to Norwich, and I moved there, too. We were in temporary offices in Lower Clarence Road while the new Head Office at 79, Thorpe Road was built (like the adjacent garage at Cremorne Lane) by George H Kenny & Son of Ipswich.

"I lodged nearby, at 41, Beatrice Road. When Monica and I married in 1933, we set up home at Hill House Road' (where Tramways buses and, in due course, the 92 zig-zagged up the hill) 'and where I was about ten minutes away from Head Office. I was chief cost clerk in those days, costing petrol, oil, uniforms, everything! I transferred to accounts for a while, but returned to stores costing and eventually became Chief Storekeeper. When we moved to Cotman Road in 1948 I was even nearer to my office and would be called out at week-ends to open the stores if parts were required urgently."

Jack Brereton retired from the Company in 1968 - the year I returned. The final section of his reflections is poignant, but also reveals a nobleness of spirit. "Monica and I enjoyed more happy

106. The operations of Robertson of Stalham, a Broads village, were acquired by Eastern Counties in July 1936. Bedford WLB NG 1979 escaped by a few days, being sold to an operator at East Dereham the same month. Could it perhaps have been the machine which conductor Fred Eagling nursed back to Stalham ...?

years together until her death in January 1978. Then began the worst period of my life. I often wonder why I have been spared for so long, and can only think and hope that perhaps it has been to encourage others who have had to face the same experiences of loss and despair that I have had to endure."

A touching and fascinating footnote exists to Jack's story. Billy Graham, the evangelist (by now, obviously, a much older man) held a short evangelistic campaign in Norwich in June 1984. Jack Brereton, at the age of 80, went alone to one meeting and made a profession of faith. It was extraordinary that the same channel was used to bring blessing to us both. It's never too late to find new light. But I count myself fortunate that I nailed my colours to the mast at the age of 15, when the possibility of a lifetime of Christian discipleship lay before me.

Driver Fred Eagling worked on the coaches, and was well-known and popular. His career commenced with Robertson of Stalham, taken over by Eastern Counties in 1936. Interestingly, at a board meeting on 25th September 1928 the United directors had decided that the purchase of Robertson's Bus Services, Stalham, was to be negotiated, price not to exceed £250. Mr Robertson seems to have expected a higher figure.

Fred Eagling was a youthful conductor when, one day, his bus broke down on the way back to Stalham from Norwich, and his driver went to summon a replacement vehicle. While he was away, young Fred managed to start the bus and, egged on by the passengers, drove it the rest of the way to Stalham. The next morning he was called to Mr Robertson's office; the proprietor was wearing his customary pince-nez. "Well, Eagling, what's this I hear?" Fred thought he was going to get the sack - but Mr Robertson continued: "You used your initiative and got the people home. I'm giving you a rise of half-a-crown!"

After the death of his first wife, Fred found great happiness in his marriage (at Cringleford Church, in 1976) to Peggy Sampson, whom he had known for many years through their involvement in Staff Welfare meetings. They were in church together - and, plainly, very happy - when I preached at St Peter's, Cringleford on 15th January 1978, and both retired that year. Fred died on 4th April 1993.

I talked with Peggy again a few years ago, intrigued at her family connection to the earliest days of the name that has dominated my conscious mind for as long as I can remember: 'Eastern Counties'. She was born at Gorleston-on-Sea in 1918. A relation of her mother's was manager of the Ancient House bookshop at Ipswich when, one day in 1919, Mr Worssam, of the nascent Eastern Counties Road Car Company, went into the shop to order stationery.

Knowing that Claud Sampson was looking for work, "John asked Mr Worssam if he had any vacancies for clerks. It so happened that he was looking for a senior clerk, and Dad got the job, beginning a period of service which was to last until 1953. I was twelve when we moved to Norwich in April 1931, and I've lived in Cringleford ever since.... I joined the Company in 1941 .... I remember when you worked at Cremorne Lane. Arthur Lay, the Body Shop Superintendent, once said to me, 'That boy is a good boy. He doesn't mind telling you what he believes.'"

Those cordial words - reaching, as it were, from beyond the grave - touched me. They had not been spoken of me as I am, but of a fair-haired youth crammed with innocence and optimism. Peggy concluded: "Between us, Dad, Fred, and I completed over a century of service to the company." Well over! I made it nearer 115.

19. Present mirth

I noted that - among all the jokes and stories and memories - tales of amorous derring-do (prominent within this vigorous oral tradition) invariably went down particularly well. Of these, there was seldom any shortage, on the buses. After careful thought, I decided reluctantly there was no need to include representative examples of the genre (although the jealous coalman who blocked a country lane with his lorry to catch the driver he suspected of making frequent and unauthorised stops I found almost irresistible). Instead, I have three favourite stories to record, none of which involves me personally, but each of which possesses a distinctive East Anglian flavour.

John Lebbon had been up very early. As his shift ended, his spirits rose accordingly. As he booked off, he couldn't resist sticking his head around the door of the conductors' room, where the late shift (with little evident enthusiasm) were glumly writing out their waybills and preparing to commence work. "I thought I'd just let you know, I'm now going home!" he called cheerily - before withdrawing hastily.

Many hours later, he was in bed and in a very deep sleep. At last, the noise penetrated his reluctant brain… the phone was ringing. He hauled himself from a warm bed, and reached for the phone,

"Hello?", he muttered, shaking with cold, head fuddled and confused.

"Hello?" The voice on the other end was indecently bright and chirpy. "I thought I'd just let you know, I'm now going home!" And the phone went dead.

Long before drinking-and-driving attracted the odium it rightly merits, drinking on duty was still against the rules. The evening bus from Thorpe Station arrived at Drayton 'Red Lion' on Service 29A. The conductor hurried in and ordered two pints. The landlord was alarmed and gave a secret warning - for a trap had been set. Two inspectors sat waiting in the corner. The conductor didn't flinch. "And a packet of Woodbines, please," he said. He put the Woodbines in his pocket, scooped up the two pints of mild, carried them to the table where the inspectors were poised to pounce, set them down with 'Your very good health, gentlemen', and walked out. The incident was never mentioned. (This story was preserved by Driver Bob Grand.)

The nuances are sometimes more subtle, and occasionally slightly darker; but no-one was hurt in the following incident. I knew the crew; they were quintessential Norwich characters. It is my favourite story.

A woman attempted to board the open-platform of a double-decker as it drew away from the bus stop at 'The Earl of Leicester', on Dereham Road in Norwich. She slipped and fell. The conductor rang three bells - the emergency signal - and leapt to the woman's assistance, ticket machine and cash bag trailing behind him. The bus braked sharply to a halt. The driver pulled on the handbrake and climbed from the cab to find the woman back on her feet, looking sheepish, and his mate some distance away, bent over a puddle.

107. Arthur Lay, the Body Shop Superintendent at Main Works, stood authoritatively in front of VG 5543 (HLG 6) for this photograph. The occasion was the completion of the vehicle's conversion to open-top in 1952, and the retention of the original pattern of cab front was notable. The same bus in its covered-top form is shown on pages 1 and 15.

108. At Drayton, the Red Lion has long competed with the nearby Cock Inn, from which C W Neve commenced the Drayton - Norwich bus service in 1922 before selling it to Russell Dunham in 1923. Mr Neve later moved across the road to become landlord of the Red Lion, where his name is seen in large letters above the porch of the nearer building in this picture. The 29A bus waiting for time is Eastern Counties NG 2732 (A 197) of 1932. (Jarrold & Sons Ltd)

RED LION, DRAYTON J & S 535

"What's up with her?" grunted the driver, a man of few words.

"B----- *her*", snapped his five-feet-nothing conductor, spectacles awry, but staring intently, "I've lost a threepenny bit in this puddle."

Glasgow humour is distinctive, and Glaswegians are renowned for their wit and repartee. Volumes could be filled with bus and tram jokes, stories, and incidents from Clydeside. Indeed, in 1990 Frank O'Neill sent me a copy of *Your Wee Happy Book of Glasgow Bus Culture*, published by Strathclyde's Buses Ltd. Alas, these too lie beyond the scope of this present work - which I say with regret, since laughter is the widest door to self-knowledge, and self-knowledge but one step away from knowledge of God.

Bill Tait's famous post-war cartoon in the *Evening Citizen*, reproduced frequently for its incisive perfection, must be invoked one more time to represent them all. It shows, of course, the conductress of a full tramcar repelling a would-be passenger, one foot on the step, with the immortal word, "Cumoangerraff!"

By coincidence, as I worked on this very page Frank came on the phone. And, as usual, he insisted on telling a story.

A bus from Parkhead garage arrived at the terminus. An exceptionally short man was waiting, and he was extremely annoyed.

"Ah've been waiting here half-an-hour", he snapped, "An' Ah'm no' happy."

"Which one are ye?" asked the driver.

20. The Worshipful Sheriff

For a few days, the buses of Norwich - or, to be exact, one bus in particular - became literally the focus of international attention. On the afternoon of Thursday 3rd March 1988 a double-decker on service 26, driven by Jim Pightling and operating from the University to Hellesdon,

RAH 266W (VR 266),

reared high and dramatically into the air as old chalk-workings in Earlham Road, beside the Roman Catholic cathedral, collapsed beneath it and left it stuck in a large hole. Fortunately, there were no casualties. I was working on the same route that afternoon.

A few weeks later, after twenty years as a worker-priest, I had the unexpected privilege of being elected Sheriff of Norwich for the civic year 1988-89. I arranged a civic reception at the ancient Guildhall on 3rd April 1989, to mark the 70th Anniversary of the formation of the Eastern Counties Road Car Company in 1919. This gave me the opportunity of welcoming the Managing Director and the Board, the Trade Union committee, and many retired ex-United employees, and of acknowledging the contribution Eastern Counties had made to the life of the city, over the years. The reminiscences flowed, unchecked.

Retired driver Ernie Spall, an old United man, amused me with his account of how, as a recently-trained driver, he was sent to Thorpe Station to do one trip on Service 13A to Costessey Church - and found an ex-ECRCC Tilling-Stevens open-top PE class waiting. He had never driven anything like it before, and it tested his inexperience to the utmost. It reminded me of the morning I went to take over at Drummer Street bus station in Cambridge for the return trip to Soham and found an LC class waiting, which I had never driven. I suspect the result was very similar.

My only regret was that Jack Brereton, struggling in the manner he has described so movingly, did not feel able to be present; but the evening was judged an outstanding success. The company included Bert Vurley, Teddy Barker, Cyril Harris, George Tate (a good footballer in his United days; driver of the Surrey Street lorry; I later conducted his funeral); Albert Elms (who looked so young I could scarcely believe he was a United man; I conducted his funeral on 12th July 2000, and his widow gave me his United cap-badge); and Percy Brown (for many years the Rolling Stock Inspector, possibly the oldest person present: but he, too, carried his years lightly). Former Tramways men included Bunny Peck, Wally Oxberry (whose mosquito bites were treated on manoeuvres) and Jimmy Wilde, son of the engineering foreman. Also present were John Lebbon, who received the phone call at dead of night, and Tony Lovett, my longest-serving conductor. This memorable event

109. Service 13A from Norwich to Costessey Church had commenced in 1923 or 1924 and this view at the village terminus gives the flavour of those days. The conductor is thought to be Ernie Spall. Identification of the B-class Daimler CB bus is not conclusive, but the second digit of the fleet number partially obscured by the mudguard is '1'. The most likely candidate with this type of body appears to be AH 8447 (B 61), licensed in Norwich in 1923 and 1924.

110. After the Eastern Counties 1931 merger, the same Ernie Spall found himself on the same service having to drive one of these, an ex-Road Car rebodied 1920 Tilling-Stevens TS3. This one is XA 9580 (PE 23), photographed in Ipswich. (A B Cross / W Noel Jackson collection)

meant more than any of the assembled company realised: to me, it was a formal expression of gratitude for all I had received from the industry, the Company, and the legion of men and women of whom those present were representatives.

The little boy whose mother had drawn his attention to fleet numbers, one dull afternoon forty-five years earlier, was very pleased.

My official civic visitors-book for the year of my shrievalty contains signatures which include a member of the Royal Family, a High Court Judge, the Nicaraguan ambassador, a former Dean of St Paul's, the High Sheriff of Norfolk, the Lord Mayor of Norwich, my mother, Desert Rats and Afrika Korps veterans.

But the signatures of those present at the Guildhall that evening affect me deeply when I flick through the pages of that book. C G Harris, A E Barker, Bert Vurley - everybody signed. Most poignant - and on a page apart - is one spidery, scarcely legible signature: H Vardigans (with that of his charming wife Doris). Harry - who thirty years earlier had let me 'drive' LKH 97, and who (with his friend Ivan Ames) had been such a keen photographer - was blind.

During my shrieval year, many busmen accepted invitations to the sheriff's parlour at the Guildhall, where the Sheriff and his Lady were frequently 'At Home'. I arranged for one of the monthly committee meetings of the trade union branch to be held there, in the old council chamber where the City Council met for hundreds of years. This event was combined with a tour of the building, which included the crypt where Thomas Bilney was imprisoned before his martyrdom, and the old courtroom where I was able to lock the committee in the dock. By popular request, my wife and I made one photo-call visit to the Bus Station, in full regalia.

The Lord Mayor under whom I served, David Bradford MBE, used a wheelchair. He had no recollection of ever having travelled upstairs on a double-decker - so one bright morning when I was on the Sheringham run, with the support of the Company and some enthusiastic man-handling, that omission was put right. VR 297 never had a more delighted passenger.

21. On the Board

It was not until Saturday 21st September, 1991 that I reached Blackpool. Walking down Talbot Road from the railway station, I saw a 'balloon' car cross the end of the road, and discovered I was still capable of deep emotion. It was a thrilling and beautiful sight, which made me quicken my steps in anticipation. We rode to the Pleasure Beach on car 713, then to Fleetwood on car 626. The long sections of reserved track did not possess a fraction of the atmosphere of Lord Street, in Fleetwood, which was 'made' for trams and delighted in retaining them. No 'through' double-deckers were operating beyond Bispham, so we caught car 678 to Bispham, and changed there to car 717 for the journey back to the Pleasure Beach, which gave me enormous joy and fulfilment and - like all good things - was over too soon.

On 20th August 1992 I had a curious and unpleasant experience. I dreamt I was driving a single-decker bus and approaching a bend. I realised I was going too fast and couldn't take the bend. I left the road and, in mid-air, could see the ground far below and thought, "I'm going to die". Then, suddenly, a promontory of high ground appeared, just beneath me, and saved me from the long drop. I managed to 'land' - and, apparently, I was safe. It was a vivid nightmare. However long it lasted, it was frightening.

I was very surprised indeed when breakfast television carried news of a coach crash tragedy in Spain, in which several people had been killed. It appeared to have left the road in circumstances not unlike those in my dream. It was a remarkable coincidence.

In the 1980s, the bus industry experienced the trauma of deregulation and privatisation. At Norwich, crew work ended and conductors vanished on 31st December 1983; for me - alas! - it was back to one-man operation. Eastern Counties was the subject of a management buy-out. A decade later, it was purchased by Grampian Regional Transport, the privatised successor to Aberdeen Corporation. The story of the beautiful trams which, when withdrawn in 1958, had been burned on the beach in what sounds like some ancient Norse ritual, became - at a stroke - an unlikely part of

111. United men at the Sheriff's reception held at the Guildhall, Norwich, on 3rd April 1989 were (standing, left to right) Ernie Spall, Alf Button, Russell Abbs, Cyril Harris, Freddie Rix (hidden), George Tate, Albert Elms, Teddy Barker, Fred Elsegood, Alfred Bumphrey, R Patrick, Bert Vurley and Jack Cannell. Seated were the Sheriff, Percy Brown, the Lord Mayor, and Peter Brundle, the ECOC Managing Director.

112. Blackpool at last! Here I am at the Pleasure Beach on 21st September 1991 with a fine line of 1934-35 'balloon' trams, so-called on account of the rounded shape of the roofs.

113. Here is the remarkable 1949 Foden coach JBJ 833 (FS 998), ex-Clarke's of Felixstowe in 1951. It was heading into Norwich along Thorpe Road and was photographed from the traffic island where schoolboys kept watch and made observations. The coach behind probably passed to the right of the photographer into Carrow Road, which served as the ring road and carried most of the coaches travelling to and from Great Yarmouth.

my heritage. For a short while, the 'i' in 'Eastern Counties' on the side of each bus was dotted with a tiny thistle. Scotland seemed not quite so far away.

For me, personally, events now took a turn - like the Glasgow double-decker on Mousehold Heath - which was almost surreal. GRT, as a young company professing commitment to high standards and best practice, pursued a policy of appointing Employee Directors. In 1995, after elections had been held (and although I was a staunch trade unionist) I was appointed a director of Eastern Counties Omnibus Company Limited, 79, Thorpe Road, Norwich.

I remember vividly the bright morning when, aged 55, I walked along Thorpe Road to my first board meeting: past where the Rosary Corner bus stop used to be (outside what was then a greengrocer's) where I could see a P class as if it were there still; past where the CB sang its destination on the wet road, and where the TD4s swung left to begin their zig-zag past Jack Brereton's house, and mine, both just a few yards away; past the former chapel where I was received into the membership of the Methodist Church in 1956, outside which the inward bus stop was situated in the days when every bus displayed clicker-boards; past the Lansdowne Hotel, formerly a large private house (requisitioned for the use of servicemen during the war) which had been the most distant terminus served by the imaginary bus company of my childhood nearly fifty years earlier; past the traffic island where, each summer, we watched the long processions of coaches, and hoped that FS 998 would be on the tea-time Service L.

I suspect that - certainly, at one level - sitting in the panelled board-room, at the oval table where the decision to abandon the Norwich tramway system must have been taken, meant infinitely more to me than anybody else present. We wrestled with present problems and opportunities; but I was conscious, also, of another dimension, of a cloud of witnesses, of Worssam and Sampson and Wood, and of all those whose labours and decisions had brought us to that time and place. I didn't merely feel like that occasionally. It was my constant, underlying state of mind. It didn't stultify my attitude to contemporary issues - indeed, it quickened, enlivened, and informed my thinking; but it set our current agenda in the context of eternity.

114. A hundred yards 'into' the previous picture (round a slight bend) this scene appears. Car 36 is approaching Cremorne Lane (right). Here, set back and with the corner (just visible, extreme right) very much cut off and the lane widened, Eastern Counties built their Head Office - 79, Thorpe Road - in 1931. New workshops and garage had already been built on an adjoining site further down the lane. The Methodist manse was halfway along the row of villas on the left; the tram terminus until 1935 another fifty paces, to the right, at The Redan. (Valentine's Series)

I remained on the board until my early retirement through ill-health in 2003, by which time - although non-executive - I was the longest-serving director (and had served under four MDs). Soon after I joined, the directors were summoned peremptorily to a meeting the same afternoon at 5pm. An aura of excitement and secrecy surrounded our assembly. The managing director said nothing until the hour had struck. Then, with the Stock Exchange closed, we heard of the merger of GRT and Badgerline, and the creation of (what is now) FirstGroup.

In this connection, I had - at a subsequent meeting - to make and sign a statutory declaration. Afternoon had turned to early evening, the lights were on, and the individual repetition of the declaration by each director in turn, in the presence of a visiting solicitor, created a sense of occasion and a hint of drama - rather like church worship.

During my term as a director, the Company acquired Blue Bus, the modern face of what everybody still thought of as Great Yarmouth Corporation. My thoughts flashed back, of course, to those blue buses in the school yard (not far away) just after the blitz....

With Blue Bus came two new directors, one of whom was a senior Great Yarmouth councillor, and for whom that dubious sobriquet 'a real character' might have been invented. I warmed to him instantly. As a gesture of goodwill he brought with him, one day, a box of kippers to be shared among his new colleagues and which he opened on the sacred table, filling the room with a pungent East Coast fragrance. I felt that the managing director (whose desk was also situated in the board room) was less than fulsome in his expressions of thanks; in the event, two of us only were left to avail ourselves of this unexpected largesse and to express appreciation and enthusiasm commensurate with the benevolence of the donor.

As Employee Director I had to attend meetings at various locations, including Aberdeen, where the garage in King Street still cried aloud of trams, and Northampton, where some lines remained in the garage in St James Road, although the trams were abandoned in 1934, five years before I was born. I stood between them and thought deep thoughts.

At one level, being a member of the board gave me every legal opportunity - indeed, responsibility - to contribute to the thinking of the Company; at another, it gave me no power at all! For example, the letters in the fleet numbers vanished overnight. The Engineering Director simply reported the *fait accompli* at the monthly board meeting: they were an anachronism, and 'Group' policy was… Nobody batted an eye-lid: but, then, nobody else present could have told a P from an AT. 'Group' also decided that the identities of individual companies would be relegated to the legal writing only, and a standardised livery would be introduced.

The most amazing development, however, for me, personally, was FirstGroup's entry into Glasgow. When Frank O'Neill and I were both in our twenties, went to Parkhead, Ibrox, and Hampden Park together, and dropped into a bar after a game; or when I hitched a ride to Millerston to retrieve my sanity; and, certainly, after I had left the city, neither he nor I could have guessed, in our wildest dreams, that one day we would wear the same uniform, work for the same company, and drive the same types of vehicles in the same livery. We often compared notes, over the phone; and some Glasgow buses were transferred to Norwich. Now we have both retired.

I described that development as amazing because its symmetry was utterly unpredictable. But another wheel came full circle in a manner which, to me, was even more remarkable! The Glasgow Museum of Transport was transferred from Coplawhill to Kelvin Hall! From that famous Glasgow venue, the broadcast preaching of an American evangelist had made an indelible impression on the heart and mind of a sensitive and enthusiastic 15-year-old. From the decision I made on 28th April 1955 I never departed. Buses and trams never again took first place in my priorities. I laid aside my hopes of a career in the bus world to enter the sacred ministry; a decade later, I *won permission* to be released from the professional ministry to serve as a worker-priest. As I have described, I did so because I had lost confidence in the effectiveness of the Church's mission strategies and its ability to confront, in any meaningful way, the drift from religion I perceived to be an outstanding characteristic of everyday life in Twentieth Century Britain.

Although I returned to the industry I knew (and which had gripped me from infancy) never, for an instant, did I regret or rescind my response to the Gospel which I received from the Kelvin Hall: neither did I ever see my ordination as other than the most unspeakable privilege and the first call upon my energies, in perpetuity. I had lost faith in the structures, not in the substance. At work, therefore, I maintained the highest profile consistent with not 'pushing religion', which I abhor. If I made few converts, I was at least visible. If I was tired and wanted to go home but someone wanted to talk, I stayed. (I am mindful of Thomas Hardy's wry observation in *Far From the Madding Crowd* that 'the more emphatic the renunciation the less absolute its character' - but I am trying to be truthful.)

Whenever I have visited the Kelvin Hall, it has invariably been in a spirit of intense joy and thankfulness. My philosophy, my career, and my vocation all pivot upon something that happened here, though I was far away. Space and time are mysterious twins.

But Kelvin Hall, with its Glasgow trams, has been a place of pilgrimage for a separate reason. It has symbolised, in a most beautiful, awe-inspiring, and satisfying manner, an enthusiasm and life-long interest, primitive and elemental in its nature, the pursuit of which broadened every horizon, shaped every attitude, and - in short - fashioned the young person capable and desirous of responding to what was offered here, 'All in the April evening'.

As I put the finishing touches to this book, the Museum of Transport is again on the move, closing in April 2010 in preparation for transfer from Kelvin Hall to the city's huge Riverside Museum project. Selfishly, whether we are talking about Coplawhill, Kelvin Hall or Riverside, I enjoy the trams most when the museum is not busy. (That, in itself, is a paradox - for buses and trams are about nothing if not about people.) But I like the quietness; I visit to reflect and to wonder. Somehow these shapes and objects draw together uniquely the strands which link all my Epiphanies, and crowns them: my insights, my longings, AAH 136, VG 5539, UU 5148, FYS 494, the Steelhouse Lane experience, arriving too late in Glasgow, yet staying there two years and experiencing life at its most vibrant and intense, MAH 744, years of crew work with Keith and Michael and Tony, Fishergate, FirstGroup....

115. During this quiet moment at Kelvin Hall on 13th June 1996, Coronation car 1173 is prominent in the line of trams, with Standard 1088 behind. The Albion double-decker was the most characteristic of Glasgow's buses, though far from the most numerous. (John Banks)

116. More recently, the buses at Kelvin Hall have been lent out to the Glasgow Vintage Vehicle Trust and are housed at Bridgeton. On the occasion of a 2008 open day, preserved buses were operating to and from Kelvin Hall, and Frank O'Neill stood for a photograph in front of Leyland Atlantean FYS 998 (LA 1) in Broad Street.

For me, a visit to the Museum of Transport is a vindication of childhood and adolescence, and of the Quest, which dominated them. The Coronation, Cunarder, and the open balcony car all seem to whisper: *'You were on the right track. This, truly, is what it's about!'* In that silent and blessed assurance, what is *'This'*? Evidence of man's creative mind and skill; the beauty of line and design; engineering ability; history, tradition, continuity, public service. And what's *'It'*? Why, the longing for those things! - the inner compulsion to pursue truth and look for meaning; the searching, the learning, the faltering, hesitant understanding; life; God.

22. Crich

Then there is Crich! Though I stared from the road in August 1959 - at the very beginning - more than thirty years were to pass before I would visit and experience first-hand the gargantuan achievements of a society of dedicated enthusiasts. This omission may seem inexplicable: but, in a frantic routine, it was far from being the only such anomaly. The pace I had set myself, and the sheer reality of my worker-priest commitment, as it evolved and expanded, meant that many beckoning paths could not be explored at that time. And anyone unaware of how swiftly thirty years can pass has a shock in store.

A comparison with Leeds 399 might be permitted. It, too, arrived at Crich in 1959 - the second tram to do so. On my first visit to Crich it was turning every head, having only just entered service, thirty-one years later. But it would be unfair and inaccurate to assume 399 had been neglected. Restoration had been an enormous task, hampered by missing parts. Time passes quickly.

When I reached Crich - on Sunday 28th October 1990 - my natural loquacity was stilled at a stroke. I doubt if heaven itself will overwhelm me more powerfully, nor win my approbation more wholeheartedly. Indeed, it was easy to feel that, by faith and hope, I was already there. One of my reactions that day was to wonder what it was about *buses* that I found so fascinating. (However, even in my rapture and confusion, in my heart I knew it would only take one rare new photograph to bring me back smartly into line.)

And the Feltham was out! Its restoration had been funded by British Steel and, as part of the deal, it appeared in British Steel livery, which would not have been my personal preference - but what beauty! Merely to gaze was to be inspired and purified.

My next visit (1991) was as fulfilling as the first. I rode on each of the three cars operating that day: Johannesburg 60, Gateshead 5, and Leeds 399. But the longed-for prize eluded me.

The day I had dreamily imagined for many years proved to be Sunday 17th May 1992. After a visit to Manchester (where the new trams were wonderfully acceptable, yet not quite that for which my heart cried out), I left Piccadilly Station on the train for Norwich. At Hazel Grove I recall looking down from the window and seeing 'The Rising Sun', the southernmost terminus of the Stockport and Manchester tramway systems. At Alfreton, I broke my journey. A friend met me and drove me to Crich.

There, he introduced me to Maurice O'Connor. The privilege of meeting the man who, in 1932, had taken the Norwich Electric Tramways photographs sent to me by R B Parr in 1958, and which had so lightened my darkness, was utterly unexpected. To be able personally to thank the man whose work, seven years before I was born, had enriched my life so greatly, was uniquely and profoundly satisfying. It felt like meeting Moses.

Maurice O'Connor had also photographed the trams of Great Yarmouth Corporation, which survived until 14th December 1933. I was amused he remained indignant that he had just missed seeing the Lowestoft Corporation trams, which ceased operating on 8th May 1931. Even the greatest have experienced the 'just too late' syndrome. However, I felt I need not expend too much sympathy over this particular disappointment, on the grounds that M J O'Connor had not been stinted in a lifetime of tramway experience.

To cap everything, (and with a neatness which would not have disgraced the plot of a prize-winning novel), Maurice O'Connor was driving Glasgow 1282 that day as I fulfilled my long-

117. The cold evening was drawing on as newly restored Leeds 399 carried a load of appreciative passengers at Crich on 28th October 1990. (John Banks)

118. Glasgow 'Coronation' tram 1282 was in the museum street at Crich on an earlier occasion, awaiting the first visitors on the morning of 6th July 1981. Nevertheless, after my two years in Govan, I felt that this picture with the name "Govan Cross" on display was particularly suitable for inclusion here. (Philip Battersby)

cherished fantasy of riding on a Coronation car. No, it wasn't Argyle Street - but, with every nerve and sense braced and alert, greedy as ever to drink in every sight and sensation and to hold, treasure, explore and preserve every second - *it didn't matter*.

I had three rides. To transport me, not merely to Glory Mine and back, but back to 1962, and beyond, was an achievement for which my admiration of the Tramway Museum Society, and my gratitude, remain boundless. On those journeys, with Motorman O'Connor at the controls, I was, indeed, in glory. The glory was not mine - only in the sense that I was enveloped in it, as in a kind of rapture, and (possibly) reflecting and radiating it. The glory belonged to designers, manufacturers, engineers, preservationists, restorers, and enthusiasts who had seen the vision and pursued it. In their faithfulness to an inspired ideal, I had received a great blessing.

For the two reasons I have outlined, Kelvin Hall was, to me, far less a museum than a temple. When I stood in reverent silence before Cunarder 1392, Coronation 1173, Standard car 1088, and open-balcony car 779, it wasn't to worship idols, the work of men's hands; but it was the veneration of icons.

Similarly, Crich is not *really* a museum - at least, not to those with eyes to see and a heart to dance. Here, the creatures *move and live*. So - perhaps it is a zoo! - a really good zoo, with plenty of space for the animals to roam? Certainly, 'zoo' captures it better than 'museum'. But, plainly, it's far more than either of those things.

The search for a single noun to capture the phenomenon has, for me, proved fruitless. Perhaps I've used up all of them, along the way. What I can describe only as an overwhelming *sense of 'rightness'* is the sensation which impresses me above all else at the National Tramway Museum. It is an unusual sensation for a museum to inculcate, far removed from the impressions museums normally create. Interesting, boring, fascinating, informative - those are the customary reactions to museums and exhibitions. But Crich provokes sighs of relief, delight, and recognition because there is an inexplicable 'rightness' about the place: this is how the world *ought* to look; this is what travel *ought* to be like.

To dismiss this sensation of 'rightness' as mere nostalgia is superficial and inadequate. If it *is* nostalgia, it is nostalgia of a special kind. Undoubtedly, in those who can remember clearly, an element of nostalgia will inevitably be provoked - but if the *majority* are charged with nostalgia, (which, in any case, is not necessarily a negative emotion), it is nostalgia for something we never knew. Personally, I find the charge unconvincing and irrelevant. The quiet, satisfying sense of 'rightness' which Crich gently engenders points to things that run deeper than nostalgia - to unspoken ideals, invisible standards, and qualities we know as instinctively as we know the Natural Law and understand that conscience should (mostly!) be obeyed. Crich seems to embody the old-fashioned virtues which, once learned, endure for ever. (Although aged seventy, I still feel uneasy sitting on a crowded bus if women are standing.)

There is also a very acceptable and potent *aura of timelessness* at Crich. Here, indeed, (to quote T S Eliot) -

> "…the intersection of the timeless moment
> Is England…"

except when some cars are painted cream, green, and orange: then, the intersection of the timeless moment is Scotland! This element of timelessness is an inevitable by-product when preservation (in the highest state of operational readiness) of objects deemed surplus to modern requirements is the museum's aim. I revel in any experience of timelessness, because it ministers to that dimension of my make-up which rues the passing of the years: which resents the passing of our youth, then of our careers; that rails at the just-too-late phenomenon; which dreads the sheer waste of approaching death; which mourns the death of friends, with their accumulated wisdom and knowledge; which longs for meaning, and cries out for eternity.

Riding on 1282 reminded me of the famous third chapter of Ecclesiastes, and particularly of verse fifteen: 'That which hath been is now; and that which is to be hath already been; and God requireth that which is past'. An aura of timelessness, like that which has evolved at Crich, can help us to evaluate our place in time, ponder, and wonder. This attitude of reverence and thoughtfulness - in no

119. *The National Tramway Museum provides a great day out for people with a variety of interests. Visitors on 1st April 1991 were enjoying "riding on top of the car" (to quote the song to which I shall refer later), in this case London County Council No.106 of 1903. (John Banks)*

120. *The magical aura of trams at night in darkened streets was superbly captured in this depot scene at Crich on the evening of 29th October 1995. The light from the trams is reflected on the rails and on the granite setts, and although the trams are in the liveries of a variety of former operators, in the dark they lose their differences to recreate the feel of any major British tramway of the past. (John Banks)*

way inconsistent with much laughter and good fellowship - is elemental, and basic to what it means to be human. Any institution or object which possesses the potential to prompt or provoke such fundamental reactions deserves to be classified, if only vaguely, as religious....

I warm also to the *air of authority* which, as far as possible, permeates every aspect and detail of all that is undertaken at Crich - the kind of authority which stems from authenticity. From the archives to the exhibitions, from the quality of restoration to the discipline of staff training, from care of the track to skilful overhead maintenance, attention to detail and rigorous authenticity generate an air of supreme confidence and professionalism. The appearance of platform staff, the collection of fares, the carefully re-constructed buildings, even the use of the staff (which bestows authority for the driver to proceed on single-line track) - everything is authoritative because the task is approached with honesty, sincerity, and enthusiasm, and because no place exists for the second-rate.

Authority is important to anyone who undertakes a quest. Misleading clues (as I discovered) lead to confusion and delay. Authoritative information and practice, on the other hand, aids our understanding and growth, as we wrestle to make sense of everyday experience.

And that is the theme of this essay. The mystery of birth sets every man and woman on a quest. We may pursue it eagerly whenever inclination or opportunity invites; or sluggishly, with eyes half-closed, interested in little but our basic physical needs. All our quests are part of a greater quest; and there is only one quest. It is for identity, unity, order, meaning, harmony, beauty, grace, fulfilment, compassion and kindness. Those with a narrow vision, or no vision at all, will find little in life that excites them. Those with a capacity for true enthusiasm will find that one fascination and delight leads on to another, and another. Those of a religious turn of mind might say that hints of God can be found in all things. I can only testify that, in me, the quest produced a person open and susceptible to larger issues - (or to the same basic issues more dogmatically stated).

The decision I took at 15 was, I believe, the most important of my life. I knew what I wanted and what I was doing, and, *for me*, Christianity has provided the categories I require to make sense of the mystery: or, at least, to make the mystery manageable. Others don't make that switch but continue to pursue the interests and disciplines that inspire and intrigue them. The knowledge they continue to obtain and the truths they gradually uncover are stimulating, life-enhancing, and valid in their own right. Ultimately, all truth is one.

I am particularly conscious that many modern busmen and enthusiasts belong to other great world faiths. Though writing as a Christian, it has been my hope from the outset that people of all traditions might, with minor adjustments and a few reservations, be able to relate to much of what I have recounted.

In my case, the original focus of my quest and passion was superseded, and never again took priority. But buses and trams continued to teach, instruct, and enlighten. They were never co-equal with my profession and pursuit of Christian truth; but they continued as its handmaid - continued to stimulate, stretch, and provide worthwhile and positive recreation. For instance, the compilation of a collection of old photographs has been a life-long delight, perusing old newspapers and postcards, visiting libraries, pestering pensioners. Dates, locations, and vehicle identification have provided hours of diversion - sometimes, with other family members dragooned into offering their opinions.

This collection of photographs is a source of pleasure, yet also a cause of frustration. It ought to be the purest expression of my enthusiasm, yet it seems to create insuperable problems of arrangement and presentation. It is always out of control! The photographs are arranged according to vehicle types; but sometimes I have adopted a chronological system; and in practice, the two become entwined and lead to anomalies - rebodied vehicles take their place alongside buses much older, which they never met in the shapes depicted. Other methods can be adopted. Presentation according to the routes being operated is an effective method, providing maximum impact.

Difficulties frequently accompany photographs newly acquired, which are always welcome but which often demand insertion into the collection at a place where no room exists. Conversely, photographs removed for various purposes do not always return to their rightful place. Accordingly, loose photographs carelessly mislaid appear unexpectedly, while many have never been classified systematically, particularly more modern views. The conundrum is immensely revealing and mirrors

121. The production of a snapshot not seen previously can provide immense interest, excitement, and pleasure. This picture of conductor Teddy Baines in front of 1921 CB-type Daimler AH 0716 (B 31) is a good example. The bus is working Service 25, which had come to United with the business of George Warne and Maggie May Bicknell of Letheringsett in May 1923. The signpost on the right identifies the location as the crossroads terminus at Blakeney in 1923-24 - the route had been extended to the quay by July 1924.

122. In this superb portrait at Newnham, driver Alex January was with his conductor Frank Matthews in front of Ortona's CE 4031, a 1915 Straker-Squire which had been sold by 1925.

life itself. The facets and different dimensions of human existence refuse to fall obligingly into neat compartments. Life in this world is never solved, tidied, captured or arranged neatly and permanently. If ever we imagine we have mastered it, and set our routines and affairs all neatly in order, we come across another photograph.

Identification (as I hinted) is the ultimate challenge of each photograph. Some have raised it to an art-form. Trees bare or in leaf, streets, buildings, direction of shadows (if any) - all these background details potentially hold vital clues. This principle, too, is capable of the widest general application. The investigating enthusiast - to whom no detail is too small - endorses the view of William Blake, that God exists in the 'minute particularity of Creation'.

This process of cross-fertilisation works both ways. As my 'secular' experiences can illuminate my 'religious' insights, so those traditional, more narrowly 'religious', dogmatic truths can throw new light upon the quest in its secular guises. For example: it's good to ride on a Coronation car: but you can't enjoy riding on a Coronation or a Cunarder (or whatever means most to you) and be unkind to your neighbour, or dismissive of his pain. If you are guilty of the latter, you haven't yet truly experienced the full enjoyment of the former. There is one harmony and one truth. There is one ultimate truth and one ultimate reality. There is one God; and God is Love.

At Crich, Paisley 68 is restored to its original condition as an open-topped car. When the Paisley tramway system was acquired by Glasgow Corporation in 1923, Paisley 68 became Glasgow 1068. It received an enclosed upper deck and, alone among the ex-Paisley cars, was allocated to Govan.

On 31st October 1993 I preached at Glasgow University (so near the Kelvin Hall). Friends who were teenagers when I was their minister at Govan were in the congregation. It was, to me, not only a signal honour but yet another instance of those cycles of fate and coincidence which occur so often. Alas, by now I was more than thirty years too late to see the cars which, formerly, would have streamed along Sauchiehall Street or Argyle Street and out along Dumbarton Road. But it didn't stop me looking.

23. A narrow escape

As retirement beckoned, my strength became increasingly unequal to the task. I was granted an unexpected discharge and a (frankly) merciful release. In 2002 I suffered a slight stroke while at the wheel of a Scania single-decker. With my brain not functioning correctly, I continued - with great difficulty - to the terminus. It is a nightmare to recall. Only by providence did I escape the fate of Alex January of Cambridge, who began driving with Ortona (Frank Matthews was sometimes his conductor) and in 1957 died at the wheel of

LNG 272 (LKH 272).

Aware only that I was ill, I ran light and very slowly to the garage at Surrey Street bus station which I had known all my life, prompted by a kind of homing instinct. It seemed to take an eternity. As I pulled on the hand-brake and switched off the engine, my sense of relief was overwhelming and defies description. As I stepped off the bus - perhaps a higher level of reasoning was slowly returning - it occurred to me I might never drive again. After all, my right arm had hung for a time like a heavy leaden lump; and I couldn't work out how to use the ticket machine. Accordingly, with a great effort, I reached for my diary. (The enthusiast and the historian were already taking over again.) I had to record the number of 'my last bus'. All I could manage was 564. I wish I could have written it properly:

R 264 DVF (564).

At home, two days later, I suffered a more serious stroke, passed out completely, and did not regain consciousness until the following day, in hospital. And I didn't drive again.

Thus a new chapter began: and advancing years and unimagined social change have altered the picture slightly. You may need, now, to speak to somebody younger (though I hope I might still be able to help, a little). But if you had said to me a few years ago: "I can't find much that reminds me of God in the structures of organised religion, where else shall I look?" I might have been tempted to reply: "Try squinting through one of the bolt-holes in the corrugated-iron walls at Silver Road; or

123. In 1957 there was no narrow escape for Ortona veteran Driver Alex January. Tragedy struck when he died at the wheel of Bristol double-decker LNG 272 (LKH 272). In addition to the police, the Cambridge tree-cutter vehicle attended the accident. It was VE 2040 (X 28), constructed in 1948 from the body and units of AH 329 and the chassis frame of AH 328.

124. I was more fortunate, and was able to stand for a post-retirement picture with Scania R264 DVF (564) at Castle Meadow, Norwich. It was at the wheel of this vehicle, and on the same route, that I had suffered a slight stroke in 2002.

search, from the upper deck, between Bellahouston and Millerston." Those of a literal turn of mind would have found my answer, at best, enigmatic. Those at home with metaphor, and of a romantic disposition, might have recognised, in the poetry and parable of the reply, encouragement to persevere in the quest.

And the quest, of course, goes on. Whatever progress we make, our knowledge is always partial, and we see through a glass darkly. Now, I am an 'outsider' again, without access to authoritative information, relying (in the first instance) upon personal observation. Enthusiasm has become a much more relaxed affair. Old photographs retain their appeal, although new discoveries come to light, now, only rarely. But the runes, the shapes, the entire bus phenomenon has lost some of the immediacy of its appeal. The tale is told.

But not completely! FirstGroup introduced some sparkling-new Wright-bodied Volvo double-deckers of striking appearance, which passed close to my city centre residence, along streets unchanged since AAH AHs, trams, and the 7A adorned them in previous ages. Finally, I could resist no longer. I didn't know how many there were, but in my pocket book (and in much the same spirit as I copied my first numbers, before the war had ended) I noted these details:

AU07 DXS (37156)

AU07 DXT (37157)

AU07 DXV (37158)

AU07 DXW (37159)

AU07 DXX (37160)

In a second example it was, I think, the route even more than the vehicle which left me reaching for my notebook in Somerled Square at Portree. There can be few stage carriage bus services in the British Isles more dramatic than Highland Country Buses (now Stagecoach on Skye) Service 57A circular around Trotternish via Staffin, Flodigarry, and that heart-quickening descent from the mountain - with its shunt round the hairpin bend - above Uig Bay. The last two journeys I made were on Alexander Dennis single-decker

SN56 AXR (222).

Early in the quest, when first I heard of 'the United' and 'the Tramways Buses', I marvelled at the richness of my heritage. Recent developments have multiplied that inheritance many times over. Under FirstGroup, the Great Western Railway (which thrilled me at Snow Hill) and the Greyhound coaches which criss-cross the United States of America are now part of the same portfolio. Aberdeen Corporation and Glasgow Corporation transport departments disappeared in the same cauldron that finally consumed Eastern Counties; the same pink/white/blue buses run in Aberdeen and Glasgow, Norwich, Ipswich and Great Yarmouth.

The small rump of Eastern Counties not included in the purchase deal with GRT but astutely retained by the management - property (leased to GRT on profitable, long-term agreements) and a travel agency - was reconstituted into a new company. From a quiverful of possibilities it selected as its trading name, 'Ortona Limited': and the company's registered office was set up in the street where I live, barely three hundred paces from my front door. It was another strange coincidence - and the sight of the company's nameplate creates a curious sensation each time I see it.

Few other parishioners will be aware that the SS Ortona, built by Vickers Sons & Maxim Limited, of Barrow, in 1899, named after a town on the Adriatic, and seen by Mr James Berry Walford while cruising in the North Sea in 1907, gave its name to the bus company he formed at Cambridge the following year; nor will they know of the green-liveried Arrol-Johnston, the distinctive-looking Scott-Stirlings, and the Straker Squires which were among the vehicles that once worked the Service 1 between the Station and Chesterton; and fewer still will, like myself, have learned their trade at the Ortona depot at Hills Road.

The possession and the awareness of a rich historical background opens doors to unexpected personal enrichment. History and time have interested me almost as long as buses and trams. I have never found the 'straight line' theory of history satisfying or convincing: that the past is over-and-done-with. It seems totally inadequate in the face of much human experience - the atmosphere old buildings possess, the 'aura of timelessness' so evident (as I have remarked) at Crich and other

125. *A trolleybus ride from Bellahouston to Millerston could be a spiritual experience to anyone with imagination. Here is another picture which I took when I was minister at Govan Methodist Church, Glasgow. The scene is Elder Street, looking from the church along the west side of the street towards Langlands Road, and the BUT Crossley-bodied trolleybus was FYS 851 (TB90).*

126. *Forty-five years later, and much further north, Highland Country Buses' Alexander Dennis SN56 AXR (222) was loading in Somerled Square, Portree on 30th July 2008 before starting out on the scenic extravaganza known as Service 57A.*

places, the vivid intensity of many acts of worship (especially eucharistic worship), and those powerful (and sometimes uncanny) insights, like the small boy staring into the corporation dustcart depot in Fishergate.

I think of history as an immense pool of human consciousness which it is possible to enter, experience, and draw upon. The key to entering this dimension lies in acquiring certain kinds of discipled training, knowledge, sensitivity, humility, and love. One year, in November, a friend wrote: 'Remembrance Day tomorrow - that special sense and awareness of what we owe, and the depth of our recurring theme, that the past is the present'.

When I retired, it pleased me to think that Jack Brereton and I, sharing the same initials, had between us served Eastern Counties continuously since the year of its formation. For eighty-four years, between 1919 and 2003, we were aware of every event of significance as it occurred. Similarly, it occurred to me three years ago (in 2007, when I was 67) that anyone who had been that age when I started work for the company in 1956 (fifty-one years earlier) would have remembered the inauguration of the Great Eastern bus service from Norwich to Loddon in 1905 - fifty-one years earlier - as clearly as I still remembered the events of 1956. Events which once I imagined to be distant often prove to have been closer than I realised. In 1956 - did I but know it - I stood exactly midway between CL 200 and AU07 DXX.

So, have you sensed it at all, just fleetingly, haltingly, hazily: the truth that enthusiasm is a divine gift, more than capable of shedding light on the mystery of our existence? The need to be loved and the need to relate to other human beings are both recognised universally. But we also crave glimpses of meaning, and look continually for patterns which help to make sense of this experience called 'life', for which none of us volunteered. It doesn't all have to come in a temple, church, or mosque-shaped package. It can come through an honest, reverent, inquiring exploration of any part of the creation. Colours, shapes, mathematics, physics and chemistry are the same, whatever the discipline in which we encounter them. And human nature, too, has a universal quality: history, laughter, ambition, generosity, courtesy, kindness, and hard work are important, whatever their context. The small child who watched and stared has become an old man. While, gradually, that change took place, the buses kept roaring past, and a few trams, too! With a lifetime of memories and experiences (to help him interpret what he sees) the old man still watches, still stares.

If, in heaven, when all the important matters have been dealt with, there is a place for frivolity and extravagance, I know the indulgence I shall request. I shall ask to see one of the re-bodied trams of Norwich Electric Tramways Company painted in the livery of Eastern Counties, by whom they were all acquired. The *buses* were soon placed in red livery but not the trams. I made early and hopeful inquiries: but it didn't happen. (Their fate, of course, was sealed.)

Therefore, even if a tram full of chickens or garden tools but, otherwise, capable of full restoration came miraculously to light, this fantasy could never be indulged, here on earth. Historical accuracy is the chief source of authority and authenticity, and thus non-negotiable.

Usually! But I had imagined it so clearly, and it looked good. Public transport in the streets of Norwich *should* be red. That had been my experience, and that remains my verdict. United had declared it and, although Hitler had forced some adjustments, those were aberrations: the trams should have complied, and been repainted accordingly. Red was the colour, relieved with cream, marked out in black, and EASTERN COUNTIES displayed on the side. Clicker-boards were too much to hope for - even I realised that would be going too far.

But what letters would be used in the fleet number? T was already allocated to Star Flyers, because S had been allotted to the Midland Red SOS types. In any case, T was a bit too obvious, like the puerile DD (for double-decker!) allocated to the Leyland Olympians not long before the old numbering system crashed. (A system so ignorant of its own history and impervious to its own traditions and ethos deserved to end.) No, the trams could be the exception that proved the rule. Lettering in their fleet numbers would be a superfluous gilding of the lily. A number alone, in that flowing, old-fashioned style, would be more than sufficient.

I shall arrange it.

127. The crowds turned out on 29th August 1905 to see the start of the Great Eastern Railway's *Norfolk bus services in the village of Loddon. CL 200 was one of twelve built in the railway's workshops in Stratford, London. The operations to Norwich and to Beccles passed to United on 8th August 1920, with three 1919 Thornycroft vehicles, and became Service 17.*

128. I marked the significance of the two periods of 51 years by taking this picture of AU07 DXX *(37160) crossing Fye Bridge in 2007 on the 16 to Costessey. Although a typically poor photograph, it is only a few yards from my home, it features the local pub, and above it the top of the tower of St Clement's church is just visible. Here is the key to our enthusiasms - everything is connected!*

24. Relief

"There's a relief, behind", the conductor would shout reassuringly as the packed service car went past without stopping, long ago, when buses were full. Sometimes there was; sometimes there wasn't. This section is the relief car, sent to collect more of the reflections clamouring, like anxious intending passengers, for permission to clamber aboard.

All my infant wartime memories of grey buses among the red are of a piece with a host of other contemporary impressions: of searchlights, dug-outs, barrage balloons, prisoners-of-war, droning aircraft, wailing sirens, American servicemen, jeeps, bomb-sites and black-out curtains.

None of these seemed in the least remarkable. This was my world; I knew no other. I certainly had no knowledge of beautiful, cream-coloured coaches. Then Peace - with Victory stamps, and a certificate from the King thanking me for my efforts - brought the LJs back to life, and some of the pre-war long-distance express services were re-instated (or, to me, inaugurated). I marvelled at the discovery that these services possessed not numbers, but letters.

The E (London) operated daily throughout the year. When it pulled out of the Bus Station, it set off on a journey to a city I knew (albeit only through newsreels, books, and newspapers). It was off to visit Big Ben, St Paul's Cathedral, and Buckingham Palace, where the King who had thanked me lived with his Queen (whom I would meet, but not for forty years). I, myself, did not reach London until 1956.

But it was the summer week-end services which stimulated my imagination wildly. They were endowed with a mystique their letters still evoke. They passed close to my house; I didn't need even to go to the Bus Station to see them. Service S (Newcastle), Service L (Leicester) and Service N (Birmingham) - to each of which I have referred - were bound for exotic and distant destinations of which I had heard, but knew nothing. At these coaches I could only stare and wonder, in a manner utterly different from the intimate and affectionate way I regarded buses on Service 92. Their effect on me symbolised the innocence and the aspirations of small children.

One trivial but revealing incident, which can be dated accurately to within a few days, provides another illustration of the intensity of this childhood enthusiasm. I attended junior school from 1947 to 1951. My teachers for those successive years were Miss Howes, Mrs Ellis, Miss Smith, Miss Pratt. Mrs Ellis failed to arrive one morning. She appeared the next day with a shocking cut and severe bruising above her left temple. She had alighted from the Service 80 (from Colman Road) outside the greengrocer's and, a few steps later, had tripped and struck her head on one of the fluted, Victorian street bollards, over which we used to leap-frog.

My story concerns Miss Smith, and therefore relates to the school year 1949-50. One morning in March, Miss Smith instructed us to get out our exercise books, start a fresh page, and write the date on the top line. Miss Smith could be stern. My mind, however, was plainly on other things as I took up my pencil and dreamily wrote: (I can't recall the exact day) -

Monday 6th M ^{arch} H 1950.

I viewed my work, neat and distinctive, with no little satisfaction. The source of my calligraphic inspiration will be all too obvious to those who have stayed the course: E_{astern countie}S, my fount of all ultimate authority.

I came down to earth suddenly when Miss Smith decided to inspect our work before proceeding further. At each desk, she stopped to make critical comments. As she drew nearer (and being provoked, seemingly, more and more by each successive scholar) I realised with a sinking heart that I had made a strategic error of exceptional magnitude, and there was no escape. (It would be twenty years before I experienced again this sensation of being trapped. At the traffic lights on Foundry Bridge, running early to get a tea, I spotted the inspector waiting in Thorpe Station yard. There was nowhere to hide. Unmoved, the lights followed their relentless sequence. Helpless, I moved reluctantly to my doom.)

When the dreaded moment arrived, Miss Smith glanced down at my work, gave a strange little cry, and slapped my head. When I attempted to answer her question and explain, she slapped it again.

129. *A war-time ambience finds expression in this view of Castle Meadow, Norwich, in 1944. Leyland TD2 NG 2723 (A 188) is bound for Earlham Road on Service 80 and retains its red livery. Behind, looming sombre in grey livery, one of the ex-Tramways LG class is dealing with a long queue of intending passengers heading for Unthank Road. (Frank Neal)*

130. *A favourite vehicle type on a favourite route gives maximum pleasure to the enthusiast, and the two are combined here. Bristol JO5G coach BVF 111 (LJ 461) at Doncaster about 1951 was working a high season journey on Service S from Lowestoft to Newcastle. There are at least two relief coaches, GVF 533 (AS 959) behind, and (right) a KNG-registered Bristol L5G. (Maurice Doggett)*

It must have been one of those rhetorical questions, to which no reply was necessary. Grown-ups are hard to understand. It was jolly unfair. Miss Smith must have been in a bad mood that day. Had I known, then, the words of the Psalmist, I would have endorsed them, heartily: 'I have more understanding than my teachers' (Psalm 119 v.99). I was ten. On this occasion, enthusiasm had led to a misguided excess of zeal, and I had paid the price.

Looking back (with tongue in cheek) it occurs to me that - with only one short word to write - my mistake lay in not knowing that the correct style would have followed the UNITED method, thus: MARCH .... Something tells me Miss Smith would not have appreciated that form of heading, either.

To the same small boy was granted, five months later, the Vision on the Heath. That he should go on to seek employment with the chief focus of his passion was further testimony to the strength of his enthusiasm. While others, leaving school, went into insurance or the RAF, my heaven was to work beside Alec at Surrey Street.

But Wednesday 26th June 1957 was a terrible day. Alec was reversing one of the Bedford Vega coaches - BV 860 - in the garage when he knocked down and seriously injured a long-serving driver, Bert Savory. Alec was distraught. I've never forgotten the advice given to me that day by J W Robson, the Area Engineer: "When you're in the garage, laddie, look where you're going, and go where you're looking."

It was sound advice, capable of wide application. Open-eyed, I walked through Handsworth, Govan, and the strange, haunting Fens. Life contains endless 'What ifs…?' What if the church had granted me in Glasgow, in 1965, the permission to experiment with a 'worker-priest' type of ministry which it granted just three years later in 1968? Questions like these are for eternity.

Shortly after transferring from Ely to Norwich I hit, not a bridge, but a pub - and still feel aggrieved. Secretly, I've always believed it was the pub's fault! In 1969 the buses to Hellesdon (and Cromer) left the city via Colegate, turning right into Duke Street. On that day, roadworks had narrowed the junction. To make the right turn I had to mount the pavement, doing so very slowly and exercising extreme care.

Suddenly came the sound of breaking glass. I stopped instantly, and stared into my offside mirror. Relief! I was nowhere near the building. False alarm! Cautiously, I moved forward again. This time, the sound of crashing glass came even louder: yet I was still watching the space between the bus and the building! When I opened the cab door, the awful truth was revealed. The corner of 'The Golden Star' was gabled. Above the ground floor (which I had been watching in my mirror so carefully) the building jutted out another foot - and upon it I had impaled one of the few illuminated side advertisement panels to be found on Eastern Counties buses.

"Sorry about that", I muttered to the landlord, who had run out into the street. To his relief, the building had suffered little damage.

"That's all right", he replied, "- so long as you don't knock the bar down!"

'The Golden Star' still stands. Adjoining it is the office of Ortona Limited....

When, in trepidation, I was elected to a two-year term as Branch Chairman of our trade union, I entered office in tandem with a new and equally untested Branch Secretary, Ray Ford. We supported each other. He proved a man of outstanding ability - a trade unionist whose advice was eventually often sought by the Company. My enthusiasm led me to no more talented person. R H G Ford continued in office for thirty years, during a period of unparalleled upheaval in the bus industry, and was awarded the MBE.

I alight from the relief with three vignettes:

Tony Worman was killed in a motor-cycle accident. He was not a United veteran. He was young, popular, and a useful opening batsman. The maximum number of busmen consistent with maintaining the timetabled service formed a long guard of honour at the crematorium, then packed the building to overflowing. It was what, in other circumstances, we would have called 'a full standing load'. Every possible vantage-point was occupied; busmen stood on every side; it was like conducting a funeral in the round - but the impact was immense.

On 8th November 2000, at the request of my Managing Director, I spoke at a directors' conference on the subject of 'Motivation'. My address was entitled 'Sticks and Carrots, Wind and

131. This is the Duple-bodied Bedford SBO PPW 860 (BV 860) which was involved in an accident while reversing in Surrey Street garage in 1957. It was one of a batch of eighteen delivered in 1954. (Maurice Doggett)

132. In a rare view of buses in Colegate, Norwich, which ceased to form part of any route in the early 1970s, Bristol KSW5G MAH 307 (LKH 307) was waiting to turn right into Duke Street on Service 87 to Hellesdon. Behind it, one of the Cromer-based LFS class on Service 10 was loading at the bus stop of which only a ring of steel now survives, while a second LFS has come into view. On the extreme left is The Golden Star.

Sun', and my audience listened to a bus driver with careful attention and, possibly, slight surprise. Afterwards, one particularly cordial letter of thanks came from Birmingham, where such wonderful things had happened at Easter, forty-seven years earlier.

I help to care for an ancient church which the Norwich busmen have used occasionally for trade union meetings when no other hall has been available. I have addressed them there, where their first branch banner, made from old destination blind material, is laid up.

The crematorium, the conference centre, the packed union meeting in a mediaeval church - beware of enthusiasm. You don't know where it might lead. It might not lead to God; but it might!

"Pass right down the car, please!"

133. One afternoon in August 1959 I took this photograph of GPW 365 (AP 365), a 1948 Leyland PD1A, on Service 10. The bus was emerging from Horsford Lane into St Faiths village, and the view of the surrounding countryside makes clear why this vicinity had been chosen for the building of an airfield.

25. Second relief

Some peak-time journeys used to require more than one double-decker relief. The twenty-to-six Service 10 from Norwich to Cromer (the United number had then survived nearly forty years) was just one working which attracted passengers in numbers difficult to imagine half-a-century later.

When first I went courting, often I found it necessary to cycle to the village of St Faiths, immediately after work. I recall - with astonishing clarity and no little emotion - waiting, unseen, in rural darkness, with the Pleiades and the Plough twinkling brightly, but with no street lighting other than the patches which escaped from the telephone box, the shop, and a few uncurtained windows. As I waited, I watched as, one by one, the service car and its reliefs dashed through the village (which, today, boasts a bypass) in a simple drama perhaps only an enthusiast could recognise and appreciate.

With an Advent-like thrill of expectation, sharp ears would catch the distant approach of the service car as it roared down Horsford Lane. This part of the route was, essentially, a diversion. The old Norwich Road, used by United since 1919, had vanished beneath a new aerodrome at the beginning of the war, never to be reinstated. At St Faiths Points (or 'The Firs'), the Service 10 now bore left and proceeded along the Holt Road (Service 25) to Horsford 'Crown' before turning sharp right down a long, narrow lane (which had been made one-way) to rejoin its original route in St Faiths village. (Drayton Lane had become one-way in the opposite direction.)

134. The rebodied 1933 Leyland TD2 Service 10 bus in Surrey Street bus station was NG 3868, which had a full standing load for Cromer before the driver had climbed aboard, thus demonstrating the need to run a relief vehicle. The bus had recently been renumbered from A 207 to A 18 to make space, in sequence, for new Lodekka LKD 207 which entered service on 1st May 1958.

Drifting across fields freshly ploughed, the faint sound could be lost for a breathless, alarming instant whenever the wind veered slightly. Had I imagined it? Then it would return, louder and unmistakable, and would continue to increase in volume until, in an explosion of noise and light, the packed double-decker would burst into view to my left, beyond the churchyard wall, and come to a halt opposite the old weavers' cottages in Church Row and beside the porch of St Mary and St Andrew.

As passengers alighted, Cromer car LKD 193 (for example) would wait patiently as if catching its breath, engine ticking over. It had fought its way out of the city through the rush-hour traffic; the first quarter of the journey was completed. But it knew it was being pursued, and mustn't linger....

Held briefly in this transient pool of shadowy light, the passengers disappeared into the blackness: some, solitary shapes, others - heading in the same direction - walking together, clutching shopping-bags, chatting of boyfriends and weather and football and prices, and sharing village news. The time was nearly ten past six.

When the bell rang twice, the bus awakened from its brief reverie and hurried along the village street to the second stop, between 'The Cross Keys' and 'The Black Swan', where those who lived at the far end of the village alighted.

Again, the bus pulled confidently away, and vanished instantly beyond the trees (which still house the rookery and where the snowdrops grow), its sound - at first easily discernible on the quiet air - diminishing, fading, and growing ever fainter until, imperceptibly, its distant friendly drone was swallowed up in the stillness of early evening.

Silence returned - yet the village was waiting; the very stones seemed to be listening, alert and prepared. And, soon, the sound of another bus approaching at speed was carried across the darkened countryside, increasing rapidly in volume (but differing in tone from the LKD) as it drew near.

An LKH, with 'RELIEF' as its destination, halted reluctantly and impatiently beside the church, as fully-laden as the service car. This bus was manifestly not content to take a breather. Unlike LKD

193 - which had passed several times through the village during the day - it did not 'belong' on Service 10. It had, perhaps, been on a school run, or had just reversed off the pits, or was newly-returned from Main Works and happened to be at hand, in the garage, when a relief was required.

Anyhow, it chomped at the bit as the passengers alighted, eager and anxious to be on its way. It hoped to catch the service car, and not be required beyond Aylsham (though, often, the relief had to 'go through'). Wherever it managed to turn back (having transferred any remaining passengers) it would reverse, then return at speed, unnoticed, anonymous, irrelevant; light - but darkened!

So, at the first opportunity, the LKH leapt away with a roar, down to The Cross Keys, then off again into the night, its sound subsiding only gradually as, frantically, it pursued the LKD. "Did you see it? Is it far in front?" it seemed to be asking, repeatedly, until at last it could be heard no more.

Again, quietness descended on the village. Still, in the darkness (on my secret mission) I watched and waited. The silence was calming and reassuring - a kind of silence which may no longer exist, broken occasionally by a voice or a dog, yet scarcely affected by the few passing cars or the handful of homeward-bound cyclists.

Then came the far-off, sometimes-fading drone from Horsford Lane, heralding the arrival, two minutes later, of the third double-decker to stand beside the church. It would most likely be a 7ft 6in-wide LKH, (sounding different from both its predecessors). It was, for sure, whatever had happened to be available! This LKH seemed conscious of - and embarrassed by - its lateness; when the bell rang it didn't loiter.

In each village along the A140 the pattern was repeated. Occasionally, in some remote spot, a car would be waiting to meet the bus and carry a passenger to an isolated farm or hamlet.

In this daily early-evening drama, I saw the secret, the value, and the purpose of public transport demonstrated and writ large, for the provision of adequate public transport is like mortar binding together the fabric of society. By these buses, people were carried home from work, school, and shops. The evening lay ahead. Many would elect to stay in and watch their new television sets. But others, from those village homes, would re-emerge later to visit the pubs, sing at chapel choir-practice, work in their sheds or on their allotments. A few would even return to the city on one of the evening buses, to go dancing or visit the cinema.

Sometimes, the second relief was not packed quite so tightly as the two buses in front. On other occasions, it seemed every bit as full, with passengers crammed in tightly, to 'clear the road.' This chapter represents the second relief on a night when it was full to overflowing, gathering the last patiently-waiting passengers (and even scooping up the 'runners').

Enthusiasm is endless because passion is timeless. Prompted and awakened unexpectedly, memories long-hidden rush suddenly to reveal themselves and their true significance, while fresh discoveries shed light on times past. Enthusiasm exists in this state of perpetual flux (which merely mirrors the creation itself, in which 'matter' is changing constantly). The 'then' which refers to days long gone, and the 'then' which looks to the future, are alike subsumed in one great 'Now'. The apostle wrote: 'Now is the acceptable time.' Caught in this eternal moment is the enthusiast, for ever looking for the ideal, the beyond, the meaning. Some might say: "For ever looking for God."

The second relief, tonight, is carrying a wonderful mixture of colourful characters, and all attempts at an ordered chronology have been long since abandoned. Chronology is important only in providing an overall framework. Beyond that, the experience of the enthusiast is akin to that of the mystic: the reality transcends time and space. Each of the items which follow returns to a particular area of the canvas I have painted, and re-examines it. This second relief has been put on to provide additional capacity: to shed further light and to act, I hope, as a summary of much which has gone before.

The preparation of this text has reminded me of how intrigued and excited I was by the non-standard coaches which appeared in the fleet in the early 1950s. These came from operators whose businesses had been acquired (though of those matters I knew nothing, apart from Metropolitan). I recall being particularly thrilled by AS 959 and AS 960 - the only Leyland coaches in the fleet. But, over the years, what I had forgotten utterly was the fact that one (at least) of these vehicles operated for a while in an all-over red livery (as distinct from the standard coach cream) and that the red was

135. In another Service 10 Surrey Street bus station scene, I was on hand to photograph Bristol FS5G AVF 580B (LFS 80) which was waiting to depart on one of the occasional journeys which ran beyond Cromer to Sheringham. This was shortly after the vehicle had entered service in 1964.

136. In more recent years, it's much the same route, but a different number in a different world. Eastern Counties has become part of FirstGroup; FirstGroup has moved into Glasgow; First Glasgow has shed some vehicles into East Anglia. Here I am with my grandchildren in front of Volvo/Plaxton P767XHS (56) in Cromer Bus Station on 18th August 2001. This is where DE 9 and DE 6 had lined up, and where I had waited to board the relief, clutching my pail full of infant crabs.

not Tilling red but a deeper, different shade. I was only eleven, and the provenance of these vehicles was unknown to me. By the time I became familiar with those interesting details, some early observations had faded from memory.

AS 959 and AS 960 were acquired from Mr W Rasberry of Grimston in January 1951. The likelihood must be that the livery of his coaches reflected phonetically the name of their proprietor and, certainly, raspberry red describes perfectly the distinctive livery I recall on one AS. It seems, therefore, safe to assume that - although bearing the 'Eastern Counties' name, fleet number, and legal writing - one of the ex-Rasberry coaches retained its livery during the 1951 season. All the relevant pieces of information have been in my mind for decades - but only in the compilation of these present reflections have I made the connection! Even when it is inactive or burning low, genuine enthusiasm is constantly revived and rekindled, renewed and reawakened, by random events and unexpected discoveries. (When preachers declare that God can be encountered anywhere throughout the Creation - and not merely in an ecclesiastical context - they are making much the same affirmation.)

In the Norwich *Evening News* recently, I found a 1950s photograph of three coaches on tour in Scotland. The coach in the centre - Dennis Lancet / Duple JPW 788 - was one of the pair which took us on the school visit to Derbyshire (and Manchester) in 1955! These vehicles belonged to Culling's Coach Services, of Claxton, near Loddon.

Founded in 1921, Culling's were the largest of the independent bus and coach operators in the area. Their livery was grey and yellow, and their stage carriage services operated from Ber Street, Norwich, to villages like Surlingham, Hardley, Claxton, Langley and Bergh Apton, in a thin segment of the county lying chiefly between the River Yare and the Norwich - Lowestoft road (Service 17; the early Great Eastern service) which neither United nor Eastern Counties bothered to penetrate. It can scarcely be coincidental that my knowledge of this part of Norfolk was (and indeed, remains) minimal.

My heart and soul belonged to Eastern Counties, and I could never summon much enthusiasm for the doings of private operators, whom I regarded as vastly inferior. The exception, in the case of Culling's, was the old double-decker ED 6562 which appeared in their livery. This was interesting and mysterious, commanding immediate respect; and I wondered about its history in rather the same way that I wondered about the old buses at the fair each Christmas and Easter. Unsurprisingly, mother couldn't help.

A friend who worked at the library presented me one day with an original press-cutting from the *Eastern Daily Press* dated 30th June 1886. It was entitled: 'Racing Omnibuses'.

'In the Queen's Bench Division of the High Court of Justice, yesterday, before Mr Justice Mathew, sitting without a jury, Mr Norman Bevan, an official of the Metropolitan Board of Works, sued the London General Omnibus Company to recover damages for injuries received through the culpable negligence of the company's servants. It appeared that the plaintiff, with another gentleman, was driving in a cab in Bloomsbury when the defendant's omnibus approached, racing a rival omnibus, and whilst endeavouring to pass the rival 'bus struck the cab so violently as to hurl it right round, knock the cab driver and his horse almost senseless, and to inflict severe injuries on the plaintiff. His lordship awarded the plaintiff £100 with costs.'

From another *Evening News* came a photograph of CL 9554, a 1927 Thornycroft charabanc, belonging to Fitt Bros, bus and coach operators, haulage and removals contractors, also of Ber Street.

The bus and coach side of the business was purchased by Eastern Counties in September 1939 - the month before I was born. Only three coaches entered the Eastern Counties fleet. The remaining dozen, including CL 9554, were kept in store for the duration of the war, for unforeseen contingencies and emergencies. Photographs exist of some in use as mobile shops when Bond's store was blitzed in 1942. All were sold to Bird of Stratford-upon-Avon in 1945 (whose yard I saw in 1953).

That latter year was, of course, one of countless fresh revelations (including the pale blue buses of West Bromwich Corporation, and the yellow Wolverhampton trolleybuses). I discovered, also, Stratford Blue, a company new to me, which operated in beautiful rural Warwickshire. These boyhood memories flooded back when, on Tuesday 21st May 1996, Michael Lutkin (my conductor

137. *Another coach to join the Eastern Counties fleet from W Rasberry of Grimston was Leyland PS1/1 JPW 259 (AS 960) of 1949. It had attractive bodywork by Lee and, like the Commer mentioned earlier, was also allocated to ECOC's Peterborough depot. (Real Photographs)*

138. *Culling's Coaches of Claxton, Norfolk, had their city terminus outside The King's Arms in Ber Street, Norwich. Standing behind Bedford/Duple JNG 276 was the imposing ED 6562, a Brush-bodied Leyland TD1 new to Warrington Corporation circa 1930, and with Culling's from 1947 to 1953. The 'Langley' destination suggests that it was the large private school there which probably necessitated the presence of a double-decker in the Culling fleet. (Omnibus Society 19/28)*

in 1971) and I were sent on the early train to Birmingham, then on to Stratford-upon-Avon to the Guide Friday depot.

During the afternoon we brought two open-top double-deckers back to Norwich for use on that season's city tour. I drove OTO 571M, an ex-Nottingham City Transport Atlantean, while Michael had KSU 839P, which was ex-Strathclyde.

Note the sequence of those reflections! CL 9554 created a train of thought which led from the *Evening News* to Fitt Bros' garage in Ber Street, to the blitz, to Bird's yard at Stratford-upon-Avon (with its deep blue, dead, decapitated Birmingham trams), and to Guide Friday open-toppers on the M1! Everything is linked and inter-connected; ultimately, there is only one reality.

Here's another example. At Norwich Cathedral, former canons, deans, priors, and bishops are named regularly in a cycle of intercession which celebrates and acknowledges the communion of saints. When 'John Francis Kendall, canon, who died in 1931' is announced, I am probably the only person who knows that Canon Kendall, who resided in The Close, died soon after 11.30am on a wet Saturday 8th August when the Austin Seven being driven by his wife was in

139. *Everything about this photograph from the 'transitional period' of 1931 shouts 'United' - look at the livery of this 1927 Associated Daimler PW 9881, the style of its fleet number F 81, and the destination blind - but the name on the side is 'Eastern Counties'.*

head-on collision with the Norwich - Sea Palling Service 5A bus, between Stalham and Ingham.

The inquest was held at Ingham 'Swan', where the jury returned a verdict of 'Accidental death'. Canon Kendall was the third recent victim of fatal accidents involving what were in the process of becoming 'Eastern Counties' buses. The company had been registered on July 14th, and the name had begun to appear on buses and hoardings. However, the relevant United assets did not pass to the new company until 29th September and the services were still being operated by United until that date. The press report of the accident referred to a 'United' bus, but by the time of the inquest (in the autumn) this had been amended to 'Eastern Counties'. During the fortnight prior to August 8th, other fatalities had occurred at Bury St Edmunds and Hethersett.

Enthusiasm unlocks and reveals, continually, facets of that one, underlying, 'unity-in-diversity' which the 'religious' person calls 'God'. Our varied enthusiasms - themselves often inexplicable in origin - are models for the interpretation of the experience which an unsolicited event - namely, our birth - thrust upon us.

140. God and the Norwich trams came into unusually close contact on Monday 10th August 1931 when the motor car of the Bishop skidded and collided with a tram on St Giles' Plain, shortly after midday. The tram was ascending the incline from Willow Lane, on the Unthank Road route. The bishop was not in the car at the time and nobody was hurt. (Eastern Daily Press)

There are as many valid models as there are enthusiasts. Religion itself (some would argue) is precisely such a model, with categories which help us fix handles to vast and unimaginable themes. Certainly, many models thrive in the penumbra of religion, springing up and flourishing like mushrooms in its outer shadow: church bells, church silver, church architecture, church history, and religious paintings. Over the years, for many thousands, buses and trams (like railway engines) have provided a potent and powerfully enriching model - and one which, occasionally, has had the effect of re-focusing thought upon more narrowly religious themes (which suggests that 'religion' - if a 'model' at all - should be set in a class of its own).

The difference between God-in-religion and God-in-trams-and-buses lies in the nature of our involvement and commitment, and the relationship which is thereby created. I concede and acknowledge readily that some of the most dedicated enthusiasts are committed almost to the point of extremism. No zealous religious activist could surpass them! Time, skills, and money are given sacrificially in the pursuit and promotion of their all-consuming passion. (Think only, again, of Crich.) In return, enthusiasts experience pleasure, fulfilment, and deep satisfaction.

That response, however, contains no moral imperatives, requirements, or expectations, and it is here that religion differs most markedly from most other types of enthusiasm and exploration. Enthusiasm makes no 'spiritual' or ethical demands upon us. It issues no personal criticisms, no challenges to a more profound self-discovery, no directives. Everything, in a sense, is *external*. It is about what *we* want, and what interests *us*. The emphasis is on *doing* and *discovering*, and only rarely upon what we *are* and what (if anything) needs to be done *in us*.

In contrast, God-in-religion requires - if I might put it like this - not only the restoration of historic vehicles but the restoration of ourselves (or that part of us which is overdue for an overhaul). Religion is one model among many - but it is also *more* than a model. It is the discipline to which - whatever our other interests - most of us turn, in our better (or most desperate) moments, (though with varying degrees of enlightenment or success).

141. This was the yard of the United depot at Recorder Road, Norwich. It's another 1931 scene from the transitional period with United fleet numbers and the Eastern Counties name, and Leyland TD1 VF 8515 (A 72) was standing beside ADC 415A PW 9880 (F 80). Eastern Counties later had them both rebodied, in November 1938 and July 1936 respectively.

26. In books and on song

General literary references to buses and trams are particularly interesting. For an instant, two worlds touch and overlap - and, in so doing, shed fresh understanding upon each other.

Opposite the Cross Keys (Sylvia Haymon, Constable & Co. 1988) which has been compared with *Lark Rise to Candleford* and *Cider with Rosie* is set in Norwich and in the very village described in the opening paragraphs of the previous chapter. The year is 1928:

> '(Maud) took her way down to the bus station in Recorder Road.'

> 'Curly.... drove the pirate bus which, operating out of the carters' depot in Duke Street, was trying to undercut the fares of the official buses based in Recorder Road. Curly's fare was three ha'pence less each way, which more than made up for seats without upholstery and the general dilapidation of the equipage. Curly was a lovely man, always laughing and joking, and a great one for the ladies who formed the majority of his customers. Once when the engine gave up altogether, outside St (Faiths), they piled out of the bus and pushed it bodily into the village, Curly at the wheel shouting encouragement, all the way to the smithy, where.... the smith patched it up fit for the road again.'

Remember! - this breakdown would not have been in Horsford Lane, but probably somewhere near 'The White House' or the rectory, up the Norwich Road.

> 'I took the tram to the Earlham Road terminus. The tramlines finished exactly at the cemetery gates, which always disturbed me a little, as if the terminus really was the end.'

David Holbrook's *A Play of Passion* (W H Allen 1978, pp.30-31) is set in Norwich in 1940, and contains clear references to Service 89. Paul and Monck left the cathedral and boarded a bus on Tombland. They sat upstairs, and chatted as the bus climbed up to Castle Meadow.

142. 'Monck got off at St Giles, but Paul stayed on along Unthank Road ...' Unmindful of the downpour, ex-Tramways Bristol GJW VG 5541 (LG 4) made waves as it pushed through the waters of a flooded Unthank Road on Service 89. The bottom line of the clicker-board read 'St Giles' Gates'.

'With Monck, every moment was taken up with an energetic attention to the nature of the world, what it could teach one, how one could interact with it and change it. That was how one should live, not in a passive muddle, day to day. He went over what Monck had said, about Bach, about Florence, about mediaeval architecture. He always had a reference beyond.... beyond.

'Monck had said in a low voice: "One of the problems is that people don't notice life. The world simply passes them by. You watch them. They come on to a bus, and sit down, and simply look straight in front of them.... I often wonder if they'd notice if the conductress was stark naked."

'So they had been in fits of giggles.... as people came on to the top deck, and sat staring featurelessly into space, or scowled down at their ticket, and over the conductress, who was so ample in figure that the idea of her clipping tickets naked was rapturously absurd.

'Monck got off at St Giles, but Paul stayed on along Unthank Road.'

Service 89 was operated, of course, with LGs, and is still associated in my mind primarily with those ex-Tramways LG 1-8. Perhaps this encounter took place on VG 5539 or VG 5541.

In J D Tatham's autobiographical *A Book of Jeremiah* (KIT Publishing; Leiston Press, p.35) I found this interesting war-time schoolboy reference:

'He could not wait to get on the bus and go home. As the bus stopped, he called, "Race you to the bikes", and made for the door, to jump down and rush over the road. He forgot that there was an apparatus that buses towed which produced something instead of petrol. He ran round that and made for the forge. He never got there. His rush was interrupted by

a USAF lorry. The driver did his best to avoid him, stopped and put the
unconscious eight - year - old into the truck and took him to the base
hospital.'

The American airfield was Hethel (later to become the home of Lotus cars). The accident occurred at Swardeston (birthplace of Edith Cavell - Service 27).

Capitalism for Frustrated Lovers (Tom Levick, Pen Press Publishers Ltd, 2005, p.73) is a compelling and moving modern novel, set in the bus industry, post-deregulation. Its detail and authority show it to be the work of an 'insider'! Tom Levick is the pen name of Andy Wood - bus proprietor, driver, enthusiast, and friend. Andy's insight is perceptive and courageous. He acknowledges and illustrates the connections between enthusiasm, passion, and love.

'And now as the candle gutters I rise from the table with a stagger and
your hand finds mine.... Today we have done chemistry and psychology
and played with nature's resources and discovered the power of
enthusiasm and have finished up with the result nature always intends.
It is what we on earth call love.'

Here, the mystery reaches depths beyond my present purposes. So much depends upon definitions! I've argued that enthusiasm provides glimpses of the Divine and, indeed, is God-inspired. What is beyond argument is that enthusiasm inevitably and invariably puts an edge on our relationships, which is evident at different levels. We make a fresh circle of contacts; we find that even working together at a shared task creates new bonds.

The deepest of all human needs are for love and companionship, and for God and for meaning. Enthusiasm seems to quicken these needs and, like an ointment, to draw them steadily closer to the surface. We may be sure that, as with all human activity, enthusiasm and passion possess a dark side. Andy describes the ecstasy; but he doesn't shrink from the pain, betrayal, estrangement, separation, and death. For that reason, his book is not only entertaining, but important.

Classical English literature contains interesting bus and tram references. In Thomas Hardy's *Jude the Obscure* (1896), Sue travels upstairs on a horse bus:

'While ascending to the town, seated on the top of the omnibus beside
him, she said suddenly and with an air of self-chastisement, "Richard -
I let Mr Fawley hold my hand a long while. I don't know whether you
think it wrong?"'

She didn't deem it necessary to mention the kiss! Later, Sue travelled by tram:

'She.... reached Alfredston Road, where she entered the steam-tram and
was conveyed into the town.'

Arnold Bennett's *Anna of the Five Towns*, published in 1902, includes another reference to steam-tramcars:

'Having prayed, she still knelt quiescent; her eyes were dry and burning.
The last car thundered up the road, shaking the house, and she rose,
finished undressing, blew out the candle, and slipped into bed....'

Some things don't change. There has always been an undeniable keenness to reach the depot at the end of a late shift. When Tony and I completed our last run from the city centre at night and turned to head for the garage and the pumps, the last car still thundered up the road.

D H Lawrence's second volume of short stories includes *Tickets, Please*, in which the Nottinghamshire and Derbyshire Tramway is described. It features again in *The Witch à la Mode* (Lovat Dickinson's Magazine, June 1934), which contains a vivid impression of a journey on an open-topped tram through the characteristic countryside of the Nottinghamshire and Derbyshire border:

'The car ran on familiarly. The young man listened for the swish,
watched for the striking of the blue splash overhead, at the bracket. The
sudden fervour of the spark, splashed out of the wire, pleased him.
"Where does it come from?" he asked himself, and a spark struck
bright again. He smiled a little, roused.

143. This view shows Cromer car CVF 860 (LL 60), a 1939 Bristol L5G, fitted with a gas producer trailer. The extra split-second it took to run round the trailer (after his short journey from Bracon Ash to Swardeston) caused young Tatham's encounter with the U S Army. (Omnibus Society 27/41)

144. An American army lorry was photographed passing a double-decker in grey war-time livery on Castle Meadow, Norwich, in 1944. The picture illustrates the agonies and torments endured by the enthusiast, with the foliage on the Castle Mound in the foreground hindering all attempts to identify the bus.

'The day was dying out. One by one the arc lamps fluttered or leaped alight, the strand of copper overhead glistened against the dark sky that now was deepening to the colour of monkshood. The tram-car dipped as it ran, seeming to exult. As it came clear of the houses, the young man, looking west, saw the evening star advance.... He greeted the naked star with a bow of the head, his heart surging as the car leaped....

'Soon the car was running full-tilt from the shadow to the fume of yellow light at the terminus, where shop on shop and lamp beyond lamp heaped golden fire on the floor of the blue night. The car, like an eager dog, ran in home, sniffing with pleasure the fume of lights.'

The two well-known Glasgow-based novels of 1935 reveal a city in which trams are an unremarkable and integral part of its everyday life.

In *No Mean City*, (A McArthur & H Kingsley Long; Neville Spearman) - Johnnie Stark - walking home through Gorbals one Thursday evening in 1924 - noticed that the red brick of the Coffin Building had warmed to a coppery glow in the sunset and the curved tramlines stretched ahead of him like streaks of gold. Johnnie and Lizzie climbed to the upper deck of a blue, Botanic Gardens tram, and Lizzie paid the fares for the Union Street and Argyle Street corner, the busiest crossing in all Glasgow.

After a razor fight, Johnnie threw his weapon away and ran like a hare between a double line of stationary trams.... The huge crowd watching another fight on Glasgow Green brought traffic to a standstill on the bridge overlooking the Green. The parapet was black with spectators, and the trams queued up one behind the other until there were five or six of them on the bridge itself. After a clash between rival gangs at Bridgeton, one tram was left 'wi'oot a whole pane o'glass in it'.

In *The Shipbuilders* (George Blake; Faber & Faber), Danny Shields walked eastwards along the Dumbarton Road delighting, though not consciously, in the life about him.... the lighted shops, and the colours of the trams. He passed Partick Cross and Byres Road. There was a blaze of light from the facade of the Kelvin Hall, then housing a Radio Exhibition....

Leslie Pagan told his son of the days when all the shipyards were so busy that the clangour of metal upon metal filled the valley from Old Kilpatrick up to Govan.

Danny was lucky with the trams, a red one, moving leisurely eastwards, waiting on his desperate whistle; on another occasion, from Argyle Street he went westwards on a tram, hurrying home.

A motor car, overtaking a tram on the near side, splashed Blanche's skirt and stockings when - caught in a sudden shower - she paused to pass behind the tram across Great Western Road.

Drunk and determined to settle a grievance, Danny boarded a tram going south in Union Street. To avoid explanations with the conductor (being unsure of which stop he wanted) he uttered a reckless "All the way" and paid over his tuppence-ha'penny....

After serving his fifteen days in Barlinnie prison, Danny was let out early on a morning of sparkling frost. A tram took him down to Argyle Street. It seemed years since he had stumbled out of that pub in Union Street. He was happier, a little, going westwards towards Partick....

A wild storm of rain was sweeping down Sauchiehall Street as Leslie jumped from a tram.... Whenever a tram appeared, there at once ensued a contest of ruthless shoulders and umbrellas that swayed and glistened and interlocked....

Trams and buses were also commemorated at the music hall. It was George Lashwood who sang *Riding on Top of the Car*:

> The seats are so small, and there's not much to pay,
> You sit close together and spoon all the way,
> There's many a Miss will be Missus some day
> Through riding on top of the car.

Another number, 'sung with the greatest success' by the Mohawk Minstrels was entitled *She Deceived Her Johnny, or, The Kew Bus and the Incubus*. It told of a faithless maiden who ran off with the conductor of a horse-bus, leaving behind her poor, bewildered Johnny. The amorous adventures of bus conductors are legendary.

145. Notts & Derby open-top car 9 is seen passing through Kimberley on its long rural journey in 1913-14. (Courtesy of National Tramway Museum)

146. Glasgow - 'a city in which trams are an unremarkable and integral part of its everyday life.' Car 296 of 1909, originally open-top but modernised into the form shown here in 1930, was photographed passing Central Station on 6th August 1960. This was a busy Saturday afternoon, with a man waiting for the tram to pass, others hurrying to and from the shops, and the tram itself heavily loaded, with a woman passenger standing on the platform while the conductor appeared to be upstairs collecting fares. (Philip Battersby)

147. Once again we visit the Red Lion at Drayton, this time to see Driver Vic Hammil and Conductor Cyril Carter with F-class bus PW 9901 (F 101). They have a spare moment before the return run to Norwich on Service 29A. Since the transfer from United, the bus had been smartly repainted in the new Eastern Counties livery, and fitted with clicker-boards. It would later be rebodied.

Gertie Millar sang *Chalk Farm to Camberwell Green* (included in *An Evening at the Music Hall*, Cramer Music Ltd, 2001):

> Chalk Farm to Camberwell Green,
> All on a summer's day.
> Up we climbed on the motor bus,
> And we started right away!
> When we got to the end of the ride,
> He asked me to go for a walk!
> But I wasn't Camberwell green,
> By a very long chalk!

Pretty little Polly Perkins, of Paddington Green, didn't feel inclined to marry a broken-hearted milkman; but

> In six months she married, this hard-hearted girl;
> It was not a viscount, and it was not an earl,
> It was not a baronet, but a shade or two wuss -
> 'Twas the bow-legged conductor of the Twopenny Bus!

A popular song of the Second World War, *We Mustn't Miss the Last Bus Home*, by Noel Gay and Ralph Butler, conveys a hint of war-time austerity:

> The lady conductor gave a warning:
> "There won't be another till the morning."

The 1944 film *Meet Me in St Louis* contained the famous *Trolley Song*, sung by Judy Garland, which I learned as a child. More recently, Flanders and Swann lauded 'that monarch of the road / observer of the Highway Code' in their inimitable style.

Mentioning the last bus home has reminded me of Susan Long, a young woman who caught the last bus home to Aylsham one evening in 1970. She said goodnight to the driver as she alighted, but never reached home. Early next morning she was found murdered. The case was never solved. For Susan, too: *Requiescat in pace.*

27. The new pensioners

A thread of conversation is the audio-equivalent to a train of thought! Both can lead to a trail of action. Here's an example:

I lunched with two retired drivers (and long-term colleagues) Bob Grand and David Holmes, in Drayton 'Red Lion' (to which Cyril Harris drove the Dunham ex-London General B-type, and where the conductor had shown such masterly quick-thinking when cornered by the inspectors). Over sausage and chips we reflected nostalgically.

Bob, who was on boyhood home territory, told how his father brought home a rear destination board which had fallen from the Fakenham bus (Service 29), and it was used thereafter to help board up the front of the coal-shed door, after each

148. The crease in the photograph testifies to years spent concealed in a wallet! Harry London, who died in 1985, was a very well known Norwich bus driver. Here, he was posing with NG 3862 (A 201) in a view showing the rear destination board, useful for other purposes.

fresh delivery. This wonderfully original image invoked the spirit of my own childhood, with that powerful immediacy already noted, which cuts through time and space. I had had no reason to recall our coal-shed for fifty years. Suddenly, it was there, with boards up the front just as Bob described, removed one by one as stocks (and levels) fell. Often, it was almost bare; the boards were cast to one side, leaving behind more dust than coal. This dust was kept down by the frequent application of tea-leaves; searching for tiny pieces of coal would disturb a scurrying centipede or, occasionally, one of my escaped newts. Mother would pack the damp dust into those old, blue, standard, 2lb sugar-bags which would form a black brick as it burned slowly in the centre of a low fire, surrounded by a few small, precious pieces of coal strategically placed. No waste was permitted. This memory was, itself, a vital experience - and all prompted by a lost destination board.

I mentioned next, how the 13A had been one of my favourite services, having known it since childhood; and we recalled how farm animals were encountered on this route until very recently. On Town House Road, a herd of cows being driven to and from milking would regularly confront the bus near the little bridge over the River Tud and wander past, leisurely and inquisitively. More quaintly, in The Street an old woman drove two cows up the middle of the road on the same errand, each afternoon. There was nothing to do but to wait, to smile, and to wave.

We reflected, also, that while the 13A terminus remained at the Church from United days, the 13B (which operated to the other end of the village) had been extended. When I was a boy, it terminated at Costessey 'Falcon'. (Both services returned to Norwich displaying Service 81 - the city service they joined and augmented at 'The Oval', on the city boundary.)

From Drayton, Costessey is only the next village - so we decided to go and look! 'The Falcon' had become 'Falcon House'; the forecourt was a garden. It was possible only with difficulty to imagine VG 4822 - having reversed off the road - standing at that very spot, waiting to return to the city (not long before its old Leyland body was removed to spend its few final years as a chicken shed).

149. There is not much background scenery here, but it's the forecourt of The Falcon at Costessey where the driver Arthur Dack (left) was also the landlord. The bus on linked services 13B/81 was ex-Norwich Tramways Leyland TD2 VG 4822 (AH 224), which was subsequently rebodied in February 1950.

Early in 2003, when I was off work following my stroke (and still very far from well) Driver John Rogers took me to visit the striking busmen on the picket-lines. At Vulcan Road depot, I was moved to be greeted in the street with loud applause - and I a member of the board!

These days, with my driving licence surrendered, yet another wheel turns full circle each Friday. Just as - in youth - my trade bike was a double-decker, now, each Friday, the red shopping trolley my wife permits me to push home, fully laden, from Tesco's performs a similar function and fires a similar fantasy. There are no jerky movements - the trolley changes direction in smooth curves (as

150. It's Friday morning and the Tesco run is in full swing. In the background, the gabled corner of The Golden Star in Colegate, Norwich - on which an LFS was impaled in 1969 - is clearly evident. On the right is the registered office of Ortona Limited.

though responding to a steering wheel) and, by now, must be thoroughly wrung by the application of uneven pressure. My bus routes were run in the same gliding manner, sixty years ago. 'Once a man, and twice a boy'....

With my shopping trolley, I always cross the road opposite 'The Golden Star' and the Ortona office. A few yards away a small circle of steel can be found at the edge of the pavement. It is all that remains of a bus stop. Bus services have not operated through Colegate for thirty-five years: but, from this spot, crowds of shoe-hands once jostled for the bus (the factories, now, are offices and flats) and, as a child, my wife (with her mother) sometimes boarded the No.10 here, clutching her copy of 'Sunny Stories', to return to St Faiths after a visit to the city.

The international aspect of modern transport operations is testimony that we live in a global village. Michael Glasheen sent me bus and tram postcards from Hong Kong in 1954 during his National Service with the Royal Norfolks. FirstGroup operated in that former colony for a while and, when the venture terminated, some vehicles were shipped back to Britain - and a few came to Norwich.

The regrettable practice, by drivers, of scribbling graffiti in the cab is, I expect, universal. Nevertheless, it came as a surprise to find myself driving through an English mediaeval city surrounded by messages scrawled in Chinese characters. Then I wondered about the lives of the men who had sat where I was sitting - about their homes and anxieties, their pay and conditions.

Frank O'Neill - as ever - added a different dimension to these international reflections. Although retired, he still spends Fridays at Larkfield depot where he is heavily involved in the social club, collecting money and organising events. The new, migrant workers don't escape! Mostly from Poland, they gravitate naturally towards their own table and converse in their native language - but that doesn't save them from Frank's sales-pitch and irrepressible Glaswegian banter. Trying to pick up some 'pidgin Polish' (the better to sell his wares) he asked one driver (who had a smattering of English): "What's Polish for 'pontoon'?" "I don't know," came the answer, "I'm from Croatia."

One spring evening in 1983 I called at my local pub about ten o'clock, and the barman asked, "Did you get that phone message?". (At the time, I owned neither telephone nor car.) When I shook my head, he looked behind the wine glasses and produced a card. It had fallen and lay unnoticed for several days. It was a request to ring Frank O'Neill.

To say I knew instantly would be an exaggeration; but knowledge was much closer to the surface than my infant 'knowledge' of United in Fishergate. An appalling premonition had returned and overtaken me, and I picked up the phone with reluctance and trepidation. My worst fear was confirmed. Frank and Janet's son - named after his father, the son and grandson of Glasgow busmen, whom I had christened at Govan - had died in a road traffic accident, knocked from the motor-cycle he had been astride when last I saw him. The funeral was at noon the next day; they had hoped that I would take part. I was 370 miles away - but I promised to do my best.

FRANK O'NEILL
17th April 1965 - 1st May 1983

I managed to catch the late shift Operating Foreman on the phone. Immediately, he granted me a lieu day and promised to cover my shift. Next, I phoned Archie Fraser, my faithful unpaid church cleaner who hailed originally from Arran. In his seventies, he was about to go to bed. "How do you fancy a drive to Glasgow?" I asked, and explained the situation. "Give me half-an-hour," was the reply. What goodness there is in the world, amid the wickedness and the pain! I phoned old friends from a Govan which had been swept away, who had moved to Inchinnan (near the Western SMT depot and the former India tyre factory) and was promised breakfast, a chauffeur, and a haven for Archie. I grabbed my cassock and, shortly after eleven, we were off.

Archie drove to Scotch Corner where, at some unearthly hour, we took a short break. Thereafter, I did all the driving (though Archie bought all the petrol). My mind was in turmoil. I wanted to get there, yet I dreaded the reality of being there, and the distress which would come with the morning. So the night passed.

I spent the morning with Frank and his family, and gave the address at the funeral service. The packed congregation included a large number of green-uniformed Glasgow busmen who had come to offer their condolences and support. This show of solidarity, affection, and comradeship impressed me deeply. (This was the sole occasion on which I was permitted to minister to Glasgow busmen en masse.) Most had arrived in the orange and green double-decker parked in the leafy grounds, the sight of which gave me an almost physical jolt. But this wasn't Mousehold; this was Craigton, thirty-three years later.

Our loving presence and our united, concentrated attention are the final gifts we can give at such a solemn hour. My words rang hollow - yet every one was hung upon.

At three o'clock I had to leave. I had offered my drop of consolation; but I wanted to stay. Leaving seemed too easy. Our farewells were heart-felt. Soon after ten o'clock that night, I stood again at the bar where, twenty-four-hours earlier, I had been given a card with a message. I expect I looked much the same; but something inside had changed for ever.

29. Confessions of a secret disciple

In a letter to me, the Revd Dr John Bowden, for many years editor and managing director of SCM Press, wrote:

'I have to confess that, like you, as a child in Halifax I was captivated by buses, trams (in Manchester, where my grandparents lived) and trolleybuses (which, as I remember, were abundant in Huddersfield). I'm told that one of the first words I read, much to my mother's surprise, was 'Huddersfield' on a bus indicator board.

'We subsequently moved to London, and that was paradise for buses, since London borrowed buses from all over the country to help with the wartime shortage. It was a thrill to see a beloved Halifax bus on a route near us.

'I continued well into my teens bus spotting and collecting numbers.... and I still glance at transport books from time to time.'

This testimony offers confirmation that, although the appeal may fade or be overtaken by more pressing claims of vocation or domesticity, it seldom dies completely. Many secret disciples remain.

152. The 1934 AEC Regent JX 1790 working London Transport's Service 11 during the second world war was coincidentally bus number 11 in the Halifax Corporation fleet. Those from Halifax were the first of many hundreds of buses sent in response to London's appeal for help, and sister bus No. 10 carried a large poster proclaiming the fact. (Courtesy Geoffrey Hilditch, Oakwood Press, 'Halifax Passenger Transport 1897-1963')

The image of a child taken from hilly Halifax to live in London, wrenched from the buses he knew so well that they formed part of his sense of place, identity, and self-awareness, and seeing, suddenly, a Halifax bus in his new environment illustrates my theme succinctly and movingly. Reassurance flowed from recognition and continuity. This was, clearly, a true revelation, therapeutic and enriching, bearing the authentic marks of genuine enthusiasm which can be sensed - even experienced - in its remembrance, like a sacrament. It has never been forgotten. An event in the past continues to nourish in the present.

Coincidentally, Halifax had chosen to copy the distinctive livery of Glasgow (which was to mesmerise me, a few years later). John Bowden's vision, therefore, was curiously not dissimilar outwardly to my own (though his spoke of familiarity, while mine was all mystery, tantalising and beckoning). But both contained traces of those insights, emotions, and searches after meaning we associate with the word 'God', and which many have encountered with excitement and delight amidst their enthusiasm for trams and buses.

153. These trams are holy beauties, not simply for nostalgic reasons, but because they have grace and elegance which go beyond the mundane requirements of efficiency, and so lift the spirits. They are Sheffield 510 and Metropolitan 331, seen at Crich on 22nd May 1994. (John Banks)

154. United's Bristol JO5G BHN 258 (BJ 61) was new in 1936 for the Scarborough town services, and was photographed on the sea front in 1953. It was a 36-seater with a rather cramped row for five at the back, and as Service 105 was the only one to operate on the sea front during the war years, this picture most suitably represents the bus on which the little girl sang her hymn to such remarkable effect. (D F Parker)

There is a strong Scottish hymn-tune called *Glasgow*, sung to young Michael Bruce's (1746-67) versification of Isaiah 2 vv. 2-5 - a vision of world peace and harmony which concludes with the pious hope: 'Let us walk in the light of the Lord'.

My contention is that 'the light of the Lord' percolates into human consciousness from many directions and an endless variety of sources, of which enthusiasm, assuredly, is one - especially if we strive to avoid Monck's censure, and 'notice life'.

Michael Bruce's hymn ends with a phrase of pure delight:
> 'And walking in the light of God,
> With holy beauties shine'.

Holy beauties! How better to describe a line-up at Crich or in the Glasgow Museum of Transport? 1282 possesses holy beauty and radiates holy beauty. So did FS 998 - not ordinary beauty, but holy beauty: beauty of a nature which sets it apart, inviting not merely our admiration (as for all things beautiful) but more: our recognition, our response, our commitment to something higher than that with which, usually, we are content. Holy beauty! - the silent, eloquent plea that we, too, should be holy: immersed in the daily round, yet also set apart, and able to see visions and dream dreams. Holy beauty appeals to our idealism, challenges it, and waits for an answer. It seems almost to say, 'Follow me' - the call that came, all those years ago, to young Charlie Crane. From the Kelvin Hall it came to me; and, from the new museum, it will continue to do so.

Therefore I ask, for the very last time - what are we to make of it all? For people my age, the most significant numbers, shapes, and personalities have vanished (apart from in our memories and in our records). 'The wind passeth over it and it is gone, and the place thereof shall know it no more.'

But in the telling of the tale, a scene is set, a stage constructed, a world created in which revelations are given. As I indicated at the outset, the language and general terms of reference I have employed are 'religious' only incidentally. That is the joy of enthusiasm. When 'religious' themes (like worship and wonder) are rediscovered in a fresh and uncluttered context, eternal verities shake off the accumulated distortions of the centuries, and the underlying values to which they bear witness provide their own authentic glimpses of the Divine. Well - they do, for me!

The loveliest bus story I ever heard appeared in the *Methodist Recorder* forty years ago and was contributed by a Mrs D Weatherill, of Manchester. The bus involved can have belonged only to United; and although the evidence suggests not, I like to hope it was an old one, with a Norfolk registration like VF 5123:

'The following incident.... happened one day toward the end of the last war. It was a hot, sunny afternoon during our stay in Scarborough when my young daughter, aged six, and myself decided to go down to the sea-front. We lived on the other side of the town, and this meant a journey by bus, which during the season was always very crowded. On this day there were only two vacant places in the bus and my young daughter was wedged between two gentlemen on the

155. A trolley standard still formed part of the garden fence in 2009 at the house which belonged to the Tramway Company at Norwich. It bore the inscription 'R. W. BLACKWELL & CO. LTD. LONDON' - well-known suppliers of tramway components. It is in such discoveries the enthusiast derives peculiar delight. The past becomes the present. The quest continues.

back seat. There was the usual hubbub of conversation and then came one of those momentary lulls which sometimes happen. It was then I heard a little voice which I immediately recognised as belonging to my young daughter quietly singing *The Lord's My Shepherd*, to the tune *Crimond*. My first inclination was to signal to her to be quiet, but before I could catch her eye the gentlemen on either side had joined in to make it a trio. In another moment two ultra-modern young ladies, sitting in the seat in front, added their voices. To my surprise the conductor passing along the bus to collect his fares also took up the strain. This seemed to be the signal for a general chorus, and when the last verse was reached almost everyone in the bus had joined in. By this time we had reached the centre of the town. I shall never forget the sight of a whole bus-load of people, mostly unknown to each other, singing that lovely hymn. They were days of great strain and anxiety, and as I glanced round I noticed tears stood in many eyes. It was indeed a most moving experience and I could not help recalling the words: "And a little child shall lead them".'

Miss Smith would have liked that story. She didn't know about really important things like bus numbers - though, to be fair, she brought a wrens' nest to school one day in a Shredded Wheat box, for us to see, which was very interesting. Then, again, she didn't seem to know that, sometimes, wrens roost huddled together in their old nests in the winter, so the nest in her garden ought not to have been removed. But I didn't tell her. I'd learnt better.

She would, however, without doubt have known *Crimond*. Even I knew it. It was played on the wireless often, sung by the Glasgow Orpheus Choir. Miss Smith took us for singing. She taught us *The Jolly Waggoner*. She taught us, also, another traditional song from a different part of the country. It began

> Let us haste to Kelvin Grove, bonnie lassie, O
> Thro' its mazes let us rove, bonnie lassie, O.

The 'bonnie lassie' gave it away: clearly, this was a Scottish venue, but I'd never heard of it. To me, now, it is plain that Miss Smith knew more than she was prepared to admit - although I still don't understand why it was necessary for her to slap my head twice. Perhaps it was once for each of the blessings I would later receive from Kelvingrove: one slap for the evangelist, and another for the trams!

Gilbert Lincoln was a retired chargehand, and a friend since 1956. I described his funeral, and its impact, in *The Gap* (pp.108/9):

In a brief address, I spoke openly of the deceased's complete lack of religious faith, but recalled that he was an exceptionally gifted engineer. I observed that life was a mystery to which we all responded individually. Where *I* tried to interpret it with hymns and Bibles and prayers, Gilbert had interpreted it with craftsmanship and a spanner. We were all made differently; a tool-box meant no more to me than a prayer-book did to Gilbert! Athough these were complicated matters, I suggested that we had both been engaged in something basic and fundamental to human life; we had both been trying to interpret and understand the universe as we experienced it; we had both - in our own ways - been searching for the order, the cause, the explanation, the reason, and the meaning that lay behind every facet of this physical existence. In my religious language, we had both been responding to God, and searching for God - Gilbert, with his sleeves rolled up; me, with my hands together!

I had not intended to say any of this. I was making it up as I went along. But, again, I became aware that everyone present was hanging on every word. You could have heard a pin drop. Gilbert with a halo was hard to imagine; but Gilbert's mechanical skills presented as a valid response to the God of truth was a new and arresting thought. So I pushed it further.

All the neighbours had turned to Gilbert whenever their cars had needed attention. The road in front of his house was an open-air workshop, and a glimpse of his feet protruding from beneath the car on which he was working was often the only clue to his whereabouts. Here was more evidence of religion - and *real* religion at that. The skills Gilbert had acquired and the insight he had been given were not kept, meanly, to himself, but were shared generously with all who needed help - just as Jesus taught us.... You see? You don't *have* to sing hymns.... Religion is also about truth and understanding, and kindness and sharing....

And enthusiasm.

156. The invitation to 'haste to Kelvingrove' is here extended by Glasgow tram 64 as it waits at the terminus before returning to the city from the southern suburb of Arden on 3rd April 1959. (Philip Battersby)

157. Seen pausing for refreshment on a works' outing to London c.1950 are (left to right, front): Ivan Ames, Harry Vardigans - proud of his Huguenot descent - and Gilbert Lincoln.

158. Compare this with picture 128. From the top of St Clement's tower we see Norwich's Fye Bridge in the ancient and modern city, with the 'Mischief' pub in the left foreground, the 'Ribs of Beef' adjoining the bridge, and the Bristol FS and Leyland National buses which at the time represented the old and the new. The date was 30th October 1979. (A R Wood)

159. This book offers ample evidence of the work of enthusiast photographers, who themselves remain unseen. It seems appropriate to finish with a view of a now-unknown enthusiast at work, taking a picture of United's GHN 189 (BGL 29) at Zetland Park, Redcar, in 1958. The bus has since been preserved.